THE
WRITING
PROGRAMME
8

DAVID BOOTH / BOB CAMERON / PAT LASHMAR

THE
WRITING
PROGRAMME
8

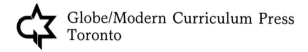
Globe/Modern Curriculum Press
Toronto

Canadian Cataloguing in Publication Data

Booth, David W. (David Wallace), 1938-
  The writing programme 8

For use in grade 8.
Includes index.
ISBN 0-88996-122-0

1. English language - Composition and exercises - Juvenile literature. I. Cameron, Bob. II. Lashmar, Patrick. III. Title.

PE1408.B668 1986   808'.042   C86-094519-7

Editor: Elma Schemenauer
Designer: John Zehethofer
Typesetting: Jay Tee Graphics Ltd.

Printed and bound in Canada by John Deyell Company
0 9 8 7 6 5 4 3 2

To the Student

If you had enough money to design and build any type of unusual "hobby home" you wished, what would it be? A fancy tree house? A grass hut? A houseboat? A longhouse? A house on stilts? A house in a cave? The choice you make probably reflects important aspects of your personality.

Designing and building your home would allow you to be creative, and would give you a chance to exercise many different skills. The final result would depend largely on how creative and hard-working you were.

In many ways, writing is like building a home. What you choose to write usually depends on your personality. The quality of the result usually depends on how imaginative and industrious you are.

However, just as in building a home you would probably seek some assistance, it is often wise to seek help in writing. Few beginners automatically know how to write well — just as few beginners would know how to build a house all by themselves. Some rare people, perhaps, are lucky. They seem to acquire writing skills with very little effort. Most of us, however, become proficient in writing mostly through step-by-step learning, reinforced by step-by-step practice.

The Writing Programme is organized to help you develop writing concepts and skills, step by step. Each chapter begins with an introduction and a model selection or group of short selections. The models prepare you for the discussions and activities found within the chapters.

Each chapter gives easy-to-understand suggestions on planning, revising, editing, and sharing your writing. Also, each chapter provides you with ample opportunities to improve your other language arts skills: reading, listening, speaking, drama, representing, and viewing. Writing is important, but it should not be studied as an isolated subject. *The Writing Programme* helps you develop your writing abilities — while at the same time enlarging your awareness, appreciation, and use of language in all its aspects.

Few published authors think about the nuts and bolts, or basics, of writing while writing their first drafts. All they think of is getting their ideas down. Most of the basics are already "in their bones," so they do not need to concentrate on them.

If professional writers make errors in the basics of writing, they usually correct these as they revise and polish their work. How do the professionals get the basics "into their bones?" Throughout this book are exercises and assignments designed to help you develop the professional's "feel" for writing.

The Writing Programme presents many approaches to writing. Not all writers proceed in the same way. By trying different methods, you discover which are best for you.

Here are some suggestions you may find productive as you use this book:

1. Keep a writing folder of all written assignments. Every now and then, review your work and see which of your writing skills have improved and which still need work. In your writing folder, you can also keep "high interest" materials that you discover in your day-to-day reading. Use these sources to enrich, challenge, and inspire your own writing.

2. Keep a journal, noting interesting ideas and observations for writing. Refer to it frequently, especially when you need help in getting started on a piece of writing.

3. Learn how to utilize the many resources for writing. These include dictionaries, a thesaurus, encyclopedias, reference books, travel folders, magazines, and examples of outstanding writing done by others.

4. Revise, edit, proofread, and polish your work. Remember, even the professionals do it — sometimes many times over. Each chapter gives specific suggestions for improving pieces of writing done in that chapter. Also, at the back of this book, you will find helpful general checklists for revision.

5. Strive for a feeling of continual growth and progress in your writing.

6. As often as possible, share, publish, and display your work. After all, writing *is* communicating!

Contents

Improvisation

Plague Years

When you improvise, you spontaneously create dialogue about a particular problem or situation. However, the moment the words are written down, your ideas become a script for others to read. The stronger the improvisation, the more effective the resulting script. The following excerpt is the result of several students improvising on the topic of the plague, a terrible disease that killed many Europeans several hundred years ago.

Not Next Door to Me, He Isn't!

MARGARET: Ooh! Oh, that's the plague.
VILLAGER: The what?
MARGARET: It's the plague.
VILLAGER: It can't be! (*General talk* — Is it? Is it the plague?)
JOANNA: Stop telling lies, Margaret.
MARGARET: I'm not telling lies. Who's seen the plague here, then, tell us?
VILLAGER: I have. That's the plague all right.
JOANNA: I won't believe *you*, for a start.
VILLAGER: But the plague can't have come here!
MARGARET: Can't it? Well it can.
JOANNA: It can't be the plague. She's telling lies, that's what she's doing.
VILLAGER: Well it was the plague in London. We heard the messenger come round.
JOANNA: Yes, but this isn't London, this is here.

VILLAGER: Could have spread to here, couldn't it?

MARGARET: What can we do? Look at him . . .

JOANNA: You keep out of it, I'm his mother, not you . . .

VILLAGER: What are we going to do about it?

BEADLE: We'll have to have him locked up, won't we?

JOANNA: What do you mean you're going to have him locked up?

BEADLE: Well if he's got the plague we can't have him wandering around the streets. (*All talking together.*)

JOANNA: And where is he going to go?

VILLAGER: Yes, she thinks more about her son than us.

JOANNA: Yes. Maybe I do.

VILLAGER: And it's better . . . one person dying than the whole village.

VILLAGER: We're not talking about that.

JOANNA: It wouldn't bother me if the whole village *did* die.

VILLAGER: No, you don't care about anyone, do you?

BEADLE: Look — where are we going to put him?

VILLAGER: It's no good arguing here.

VILLAGER: That's Joanna's job. She's his mother.

VILLAGER: Yes — you find a place to put him.

JOANNA: He's going to my house — that's where he's going.

VILLAGER: He's not going to your house — not next door to me, he isn't!

JOANNA: He's going in my house, that's where he's going!

VILLAGER: He's *not* going in your house.

JOANNA: Why isn't he then? You can't stop me putting him in his own house can you?

VILLAGER: Not next door to *me*.

BEADLE: Yes, he has his rights; he probably might get the plague.

VILLAGER: I bet I will — if you go in there.

JOANNA: So have I: I pay taxes on my house so I have a right to go in it, haven't I?

VILLAGER: He'll have to go somewhere.

VILLAGER: Yes. In an old place, somewhere away . . .

JOANNA: Why should it be an old house? He's a *human being* not an animal!

BEADLE: Well he has the plague, he's not an ordinary human being.

JOANNA: That makes him different does it? So that means you can just kick him about and put him anywhere you want to? Well it doesn't to me.

BEADLE: I am the Beadle.

(In the end, the Beadle orders two men to carry the son to an outlying hut.)

BEADLE: Joanna has taken my orders. So *you* will take my orders.

VILLAGER: *(Pause)* Come on, Peter. Let's take him.

VILLAGER: I hope you get it first.

VILLAGER: I doubt it, if you had hold of him.

VILLAGER: Joanna, you're not going in there are you?

JOANNA: Why shouldn't I go in there?

VILLAGER: Well, he's got the plague!

JOANNA: Yes, and he's my son.

VILLAGER: I said: Are you coming in?

JOANNA: Yes.

VILLAGER: Then come on in.

BEADLE: You'll have to stay in there!

JOANNA: Who says I'll stay in? If I want to come out I will do!

BEADLE: *I* say you will stay in there.

VILLAGER: Yes, now *you* must take his orders.

JOANNA: I don't have to do everything he says.

BEADLE: It's written in the Plague Laws.

(Whispering) She's going in there! She'll catch the plague off her own son!

VILLAGER: There's nothing we can do, except paint the cross on the door.

VILLAGER: *(Pause)* Come on, Peter, let's go.

BUILDING A WRITING CONTEXT

1. **How do you know the participants were listening to each other?**
2. **Do you think people would behave in a similar manner if the plague were to strike today?**
3. **What narration would have helped you better understand the situation?**

THE WRITING WORKSHOP

Preparing to Write

You will now have opportunities to use conversation and improvisation as a basis for writing. The ideas will come from the words of the speakers. Your job will be to take what you see and hear and put it into written form.

However, you should not just transcribe the dialogue like a tape-recorder. Instead use the spoken language to create your own composition.

Developing the Writing

A. Listen to a "conversation snapshot" (short dialogue) in the hall, at break, in a store, or in some similar place. Use this as the basis for a piece of dialogue writing, determining the mood and situation as you wish.

B. **Writing from Improvisation**
1. As a class, arrange for a group of students to continue the improvisation "Not Next Door to Me, He Isn't." What happens to the young man? Is he cured or does he die? How do the villagers react?
2. Students not taking part in the improvisation should work in groups, recording their impressions in one or both of the following ways:
   • Tape-record the improvisation for later reference.
   • Take notes as the characters are speaking.
3. Your group should now use its impressions of the improvisation as the basis for a new piece of writing. This piece of writing may be a short story, a poem, a newspaper report, or some other suitable form.

Revising and Editing

Because your work began as oral conversation or improvisation, you and your group will have to pay careful attention to spelling, punctuation, and capitalization. Proofread, correcting any errors you notice.

Sharing and Publishing

To help you and your group understand if you have caught the intention of the improvised work, you can read your composition aloud to the group who presented it. They may not have completely understood what *they* were saying until they hear it interpreted by your group.

Growing from Writing

Work in a group. Use the following poem as the basis for an improvisation.

A Strange Visitor
Robert Zend

The outer space intelligence
who hovered over my desk,
a glowing vibrating sphere,
one foot in diameter,
asked me endless questions, for instance:
"What were you doing before I appeared?"
and "Why?" and "For what reason?"
to which I replied I was reading the newspaper
to be informed about what was going on
in the world, and explained the nature
of money and economics and capitalism and communism
and inflation and crises and wars and nations
and borders and territorial expansion and history —
Then he asked me what the other creature
(my two-year-old daughter) was doing.
I said she was playing on the broadloom,
talking to her dolls and herself —
Well, this outer space intelligence rather disappointed me,
for after my succinct answers
he asked such a stupid question
that I suspected he hadn't understood anything at all,
the question being: "How many years does it take
for a wrinkled, wrought-up human baby
like you behind a desk, to shrink into a happy,
light-hearted being like the one on the rug?"

The players can be reporting back to their planet council on the strange manner in which Earthlings appear to grow younger and to shrink into "light-hearted beings."

Representatives from Earth can attempt to explain to the Aliens how life on Earth works in a different fashion. How does life on the other planet change and develop?

Interview

Anna's Story

The information we get through interviews is called *first-hand* information because it comes directly from the person involved. First-hand information is generally the most reliable.

Interview with Anna Heininey
THERESA MACK

The Williams Residence, a formidable sixteen-story building across the street from P.S. (Public School) 75 in Manhattan, is a Salvation Army hotel for people over sixty-five. Except for a few residents who are active and come over to the school to work as volunteers, there has never been much contact between the Residence guests and the P.S. 75 students. Sometimes, when you look out the windows at school, you'll see an old person sitting in his window watching the children come and go.

Last fall I decided to start visiting the Williams Residence regularly with a group of children to make videotapes with some of the old people living there. I found ten interested kids . . . and every Tuesday afternoon during the school year we went across the street to visit, lugging the video equipment with us. . . .

The kids worked hard. One week they would do some video-taping — interviews in the lounge, or activities in the coffee shop or craft room. The following week they would show the unedited videotape on a large TV in the lounge to an audience of fifteen or twenty people.

After a few months, when we'd taped several Residence activities and done lots of two-minute interviews, I began encouraging people to give us more of their time for an interview, to share more about their past. But being interviewed in an in-depth manner didn't appeal to many people. They didn't seem to take to the idea of talking to us in detail about their lives while being videotaped — and who could blame them, really? Many expressed concern that the children would be bored with the past, or upset by hearing the painful experiences they had had during the depression or World War II. The kids, on the other hand, were eager for stories, especially about what it was like growing up sixty or seventy years ago.

There were a few people who understood what we were asking for, and whose personalities made it easier for them to be interviewed. One of these was Anna Heininey — sixty-six years old, outgoing and very active in cultural and community affairs — who invited us up to her apartment one afternoon in March. She greeted us in her native costume, showed us her feather bed and her naturalization papers, and talked to us about her life. Heather, the interviewer, didn't have to coax anything out of Anna. She showed her sensitivity by listening, and only occasionally asking a question which didn't break the flow of Anna's story.

When we showed the interview the next week in the lounge to an unusually large audience, the room was more emotionally charged than it had been for any other video showing. People laughed and sighed along with Anna on TV, and Anna watched herself with a soft smile and tears in her eyes. One woman, clearly impressed with Anna's life story, kept exclaiming throughout the interview, "And it's *true*. It's all true!"

An Interview with Anna Heininey

H: What is your name?

A: My name is Mrs. Anna Heininey.

H: That's a very nice outfit you have on. Where did you get it?

A: Oh, from my hometown in the Black Forest. That's in the southern part of Germany. You like it?

H: Yes. Did you make it?

A: No, no. There's a lady made it. She's eighty-two years old. But the young people don't wear it any more. It's just the old-timers. They wear it to go to church, or in parades and things like that.

H: Why don't they like to wear it in Germany anymore?

A: Oh the children there, the young people there are just like here now. They wear shorts and they wear all the kind of clothes you wear, you see. This now is getting so old that they started putting it in the museums you know? And only the old-timers wear it yet — because they wore it all their life, that's why.

H: What was your childhood like in Germany?

A: Well, it wasn't too happy because we lost our father in the First War. He got killed in the First War. And my mother was left with four small children, you see. Had two brothers and two little girls. So, she brought us two girls to America. But in Germany we lived on a farm way up in the mountains where it was very cold. And we all slept in feather beds (laughs). But I went to school there until I was fifteen years old, and then my mother — she had to wait two years till it was our turn to immigrate to America. Then we came to America. . . .

H: It was different, real different. . . .

A: It was — oh yes, how different. And then we stayed at some people's house for about two, three weeks until my mother got a job and I got a job as a domestic, to live in. I got $25 a month and I got my room and board. And also, my mother did the same and she put my little sister in an institution and we paid for her there, until she got to be sixteen years old, see.

But, ohhh the nicest thing when I first came here was the player piano. You put a roll in there and that thing was rollin' around and the keys was movin' like that, you know. That was the happiest thing for me, you know? I sit there for hours — those people had the player piano, that thing was going for hours, you know (laughs). And a rockin' chair they had, which I never saw. And I kept rockin' and rockin'. And also bananas — I had never had bananas.

H: They don't have bananas in Germany?

A: No, not where I was, didn't have any bananas. The first banana I ate was when I was fifteen years old, see. (sigh) So . . . that was happy. That was in 1926 when I came, when we came, see?

H: Did your brothers stay in Germany?

A: Yes, my brothers stayed there. They were bigger. And afterwards they had to go in the Second War, and they both got killed in the Second War. And my mother stayed here ten years until we got on our feet. And then she went back, see? She wanted to die in her own homeland, of course. My father was there in the cemetery in the hometown, and she wanted to be with him. So after we got on our feet she went back.

Well, lo and behold, I wasn't here long, and I got married quick! When I was seventeen (laughs) to a man who was born in Beirut, Lebanon. That's in the Holy Land, you know, in the Middle East. And we were married thirty-five happy years. . . . Ohhh, he was a good man. I was so lucky. And we had one child — a little girl — and she died in infancy.

So during the depression — we got married in Brooklyn, New York and we were there five years. The depression came and he couldn't get no work nowhere. He used to work in the shipyards. And so he said, I'll go out of town and see if there is anything doing. So he went to Connecticut. He knew somebody there and he got a job in the shipyard which was in Groton, Connecticut — that's by New London, you know, the naval base there. And he got a job three days a week and started to pick up and then he started to get five days and so on.

And we lived up there for forty years. You know where it is, Mystic Seaport and those places up there? You never been there?

H: No.

A: Oh, you should go there some day. Mystic Seaport is great. So we lived there by the Thames River. There was Groton on one side, New London on the other side. And in the meantime, my husband died there and, uh, my sister also died. My sister never married. She was a domestic all her life because she was sickly all her life. And she also died and they both are buried in Connecticut, where I'll also go eventually. That's in Fairfield, Connecticut, see.

And, uh . . . anyway, then I was left alone and it was kind of lonely up there in the country alone, so I says, "Well, now I'll go to 'fun city'. I'll go to New York and I'm going to settle there." Which I did — I made the application here to the Salvation Army, and here I am now two and a half years and I like it very much. . . . I have a nice old age. Have a miserable youth, but I got a nice old age.

BUILDING A WRITING CONTEXT

1. **Why were some people at the Residence reluctant to be interviewed? How do you think an interviewer can help an interviewee feel at ease?**
2. **If you could ask Anna Heininey two questions, what would they be?**

THE WRITING WORKSHOP

Preparing to Write

Interviews can be used for a variety of purposes. The objective may be to get information for one of the following.

1. **Profile.** The personality of the person being interviewed is the focus of this interview. While the person's work or hobby may also be discussed, the main focus is on the person as an individual.
2. **Report.** The purpose of this interview is to obtain information to share with other people in either a written or oral report. The person being interviewed is usually an expert in the field, or is in charge of the needed information; for example, a librarian. This type of interview can be used effectively as part of a research project.
3. **Argument.** The purpose of this interview is to build the basis for an argument. The person being interviewed may be quoted as an authority, and his or her statements will help to back up the argument. This type of interview can be

effectively used as preparation for formal or informal debating situations.

What kind of interview is the one with Anna Heininey?

Developing the Writing

1. Once you decide on the purpose of your interview, select your topic and the person to be interviewed. Preparation is necessary to conduct a good interview. You can prepare by:
   - Becoming familiar with the topic of the interview.
   - Writing down your questions.

   Your questions can be of two types:

   Direct Questions. This type of question requires specific information from the interviewee, and answers are usually brief. Examples:
   - When did you arrive in Canada?
   - Do you like to ski?

   Open-Ended Questions. This type of question invites the opinions and views of the interviewee. It requires more elaboration in the response. Examples:
   - How did you become interested in . . . ?
   - How do you think this will affect . . . ?
   - Why do you think . . . ?
   - Phoning ahead to make an appointment with the interviewee. Be polite and make sure the time is convenient for the interviewee.
   - Practising asking your questions. (Have a friend pretend to be the interviewee.)
   - Being aware of time. Be on time for the interview. Plan it to last for 20 to 30 minutes. If time is running out, adjust your questions, perhaps leaving some out.
   - Arranging the chairs so that you and the interviewee are comfortable, are facing each other, and can make eye contact easily.
2. As you conduct your interview, it will be necessary to tape-record or video-tape it, or else to take careful notes. Let the interviewee know how you plan to record the interview.
3. Finally it is time to write up the interview. Use the format of the Anna Heininey interview. Make careful use of your tapes or notes.

Sharing and Publishing

Share your write-up of the interview with the interviewee. Talk about the interview's strong and weak points.

Growing from Writing

Watch and listen to several TV interviews and note techniques used by the interviewers. Of the interviews you watched, which one was the best? Why? Which one was the least effective? Why?

TV Scripts

A Country Romance

Drama on television is very different from drama
presented live on stage in the theatre. In television, there
is no immediate audience. In the theatre, the response of
the audience affects the play. The TV camera watches the
actor at very close range, even noticing the movement of
an eyelid. On stage, the actor must use large expressive
gestures to get ideas across. Television allows many points
of view and different angles of vision for the audience.
The theatre can present only one point of view.

When a writer creates a script for television, he or she
must consider such differences. The writer tries to help
the director create a production that uses television's
strengths well. The following excerpts are taken from a TV
script that the author adapted from one of her own short
stories.

from How I Met My Husband
ALICE MUNRO

Characters
EDIE about 15 or 16, countrygirl of the late 1940s, fairly pretty.
EDIE a grown woman. As narrator (voice over).
LORETTA BIRD countrywoman in her 30s, much deteriorated in
   appearance, slatternly clothes, great interest in other people's
   lives, malice so open it has a glow of innocence.
DR. PEEBLES veterinary surgeon, early 30s, agreeable, not
   perceptive.

14

MRS. PEEBLES early 30s, good-looking, mildly discontented, sharper than her husband.

CHRIS WATTERS good-looking, easily courteous, sometimes teasing, absolutely secretive, damaged, fleeing young man. He offers people his kindness, hoping they won't ask anything else. His flirtatiousness is responsive, even defensive. Women of course find him attractive.

MAILMAN shy, ordinary-looking young countryman.

JOEY 6 or 7 years old.

HEATHER 9 or 10 years old.

ACT ONE

FADE IN:

SCENE 1: EXTERNAL SEQUENCE. DAY. THE PEEBLESES' YARD.
Edie, Joey, and Heather are picking berries along the roadside close to a mailbox, on which is written: Dr. G. A. Peebles.

    SOUND *of approaching car. The children look up, run towards the mailbox, calling, "It's the mailman!", "Mailman's here!", or something of that sort.*

    Car slows, veers off the road, stops at the mailbox. The mailman leans out and hands the mail to the children, dividing letters and circulars so they both get some (meanwhile smiling uncertainly at Edie, who has come up behind them, not too close).

Mailman: Get some berries?

Edie nods. They should both seem shy, though without particular tension; when Edie speaks, it is as though curiosity, and perhaps some homesickness, had got the better of her.

Edie: Are you a Carmichael?

Mailman: *(Pleased)* How come you knew that?

Edie: Your face.

Mailman: How come?

Edie: There's some Carmichaels living out by us.

Mailman: Don't you live here?

Edie: *(Shakes her head, indicating no dissatisfaction but perhaps limitations.)* Just work.

    The car pulls away. Edie carrying berry pail follows the children into the house.

DISSOLVE TO;

Edie's voice: *(This is the narrating voice of Edie as a mature woman, just a little more grainy, confident, wry, than the voice of Edie as a girl.)* I was fifteen and away from home for the first time. My parents had made the effort and sent me to high school for a year but I didn't like it. Dr. Peebles was staying at our place for dinner, having just helped one of our cows have twins, and he said I looked smart to him and his wife was looking for a girl to help. . . .

SCENE 4: INTERIOR SEQUENCE. DAY. THE PEEBLESES' DINING ROOM.

Edie's voice: Dr. and Mrs. Peebles were nice to me, as much as they could be. They had me eat my meals with them — to tell the truth I expected to, I didn't know there were families who don't.

During the last part of Edie's narration we see her approach the dining-room table at which Dr. and Mrs. Peebles, Joey, and Heather are seated. Edie carries a salad plate which she puts on the table, then seats herself.

Mrs. Peebles: *(Indicating dish)* I think my jellied salad turned out well. Have some.

Dr. Peebles: Very nice.

Joey: I want some pie.

We hear the SOUND *of a plane, growing louder.*

Dr. Peebles: Listen, what on earth. . . .

Joey: A plane! A plane! It's gonna crash into the house. . . *(Joey jumps up and rushes out of the dining room, followed by the others.)*

                                                                  CUT TO:

SCENE 5: EXTERNAL SEQUENCE. DAY. THE PEEBLESES' YARD.

They run into the yard, looking up, watching the plane come in over the tree-tops and land across the road, in the fairgrounds.

Joey: Is it gonna be a crash landing?

Dr. Peebles: Of course not. He knows what he's doing, Joey.

Mrs. Peebles: *(Relieved, after a moment's watching)* All right. Back in the house. Let's not stand here gawking like a set of farmers.

Guarded look on Edie's face. Loretta Bird comes around the corner of the house, out of breath.

Loretta: I thought he was going to kill youse all.

I know what he's landed here for. I bet he's got permission to use the fairgrounds and take people up for rides. It's the same fellow who was over at Palmerston last week and was up the lakeshore week before that. I wouldn't go up if you paid me.

Dr. Peebles: I would. I'd like to see this neighbourhood from the air.

16

Mrs. Peebles: I can see all I need to see of it from the ground.

Heather: I want to go up in the plane! How about you, Edie?

Edie: I don't know.

Loretta: People are going to be coming out here in cars raising up dust and tramping on your property. If I was youse I would complain.

Mrs. Peebles: Will you have some dessert?

Loretta: Well, as long as it's not out of a tin. I haven't got the right kind of stomach for tins. I can only eat home canning.

Edie looks as though she could slap her. They all begin to move back into the house.

The plane is sitting in the fairgrounds.

DISSOLVE TO:

SCENE 6: INTERNAL SEQUENCE. DAY. PEEBLESES' KITCHEN AND BEDROOM.

Edie's voice: The day after the plane landed Mrs. Peebles put both children in the car and drove them over to Chelsey, to get their hair cut. I loved being left in the house, alone. . . .

(Establish that Edie is alone in the house. SOUND of car leaving; she can wave through kitchen window, perhaps children's voices calling good-bye. She fusses around the kitchen a bit, then heads deliberately but with some air of caution or trepidation for the master bedroom.)

I had been in Mrs. Peebles' bedroom plenty of times, cleaning, and I always took a good look in her closet, at the clothes she had hanging there. . . . I wouldn't have looked in her bureau drawers, but a closet is open to anybody . . . That's a lie, I would have looked in the drawers, but I would have felt worse doing it and been more scared she could tell. . . .

(Edie looking into Mrs. Peebles' closet, considering, fingering, finally drawing out the satin evening-dress, admiring it, then very quickly chucking off her own outer clothes and putting it on. Looking in the mirror, pinning up her hair, helping herself to make-up, jewellery, more and more daring, showing a sense of her own elegance.)

All the excitement made me thirsty. The Peebleses drank ginger-ale or fruit drinks all day, like water, and I was getting so I did too. Also there was no limit on ice cubes, which I was so fond of I would even put them in a glass of milk. . . .

She walks with an air of consequence into the kitchen, opens the refrigerator, pours herself a glass of ginger-ale, gets out the ice cubes, etc. At some point during this we see Chris watching her through the screen door. When she has shut the refrigerator door and turns, glass in hand, she sees him too, and jumps, looks at once to see if she has spilled ginger-ale on the dress.

Chris: I never meant to scare you. I knocked but you were getting the ice out, you didn't hear me . . . *(No response from Edie.)* I'm from the plane over there. My name is Chris Watters, and I was wondering, could I use your pump?

Edie: You're welcome.

Chris: Were you going to a dance? Or is that the way the ladies around here generally get dressed up in the afternoon? *(Edie is overcome with embarrassment.)* You live here? Are you the lady of the house?

Edie: I'm the hired girl.

Chris: Well I just wanted to tell you, you look very nice. I got a surprise when I looked in the door and saw you, you looked so nice and beautiful. *(Edie would like to answer but is unable. Chris understands her embarrassment, smiles, and turns to go.)*

Edie: *(Calling after him)* We have piped water in the house. Save you pumping.

Chris: I don't mind the exercise. Thank you.

Edie: *(Faintly)* You're welcome. *(She goes to the window and watches him as long as there is a sound of pumping.)*

END OF ACT ONE

BUILDING A WRITING CONTEXT

1. What terms in the script are particular to television?
2. Would you watch this play on television? Why or why not?

THE WRITING WORKSHOP

Preparing to Write

Creating a script for television can help us look more critically at what we are seeing, and understand how television people control and manipulate our thoughts and feelings. Sometimes we allow ourselves to be controlled by the entertainment power of television. However, from time to time, we should question what we are seeing and feeling, measuring it against our own experiences of reality.

The following camera terms are useful in creating a script for television. Using terms such as these, we can express ideas quickly and succinctly.

Angle: A special camera position that will highlight a person or dramatic scene. The director may call for the camera to "angle on the hero." This means that in a scene with a number of cameras, one camera will focus on or favour the hero.

Close-up: Camera comes in close and focuses on a single person or object.

Cut: A quick change from one scene, person, or group to another. It is common to have cuts when two people are talking to each other.

Dissolve: The fading away of a scene as the next scene appears. A dissolve is one way of changing from one scene to another.

Dollying: Moving a camera closer in towards a scene, or farther out.

Establishing Shot: A camera shot or scene used to tell the viewer where the story is taking place. A far shot of an ocean liner tells the viewer that part of the story is going to take place at sea on a large ship.

Exterior: An outdoor scene. It can be in an alley in a city, on a great prairie, in a barnyard, or any other outdoor location.

Fade In: The screen goes black and a new scene or picture begins to appear slowly. At first it is barely visible — a "faded" picture. As it begins to become clearer, it "fades in" until it is a full normal picture.

Fade Out: A scene begins to disappear. Slowly the picture fades away to nothing. A *fade out* is the opposite of a *fade in*.

Focusing: Adjusting the camera for the clearest, sharpest picture.

Freeze Frame: The process of stopping the action on the screen so that there appears to be a still picture on the set. This is also called *stop action*.

Head Shot: A picture of a person from the shoulders up.

Interior: Any scene that takes place indoors.

Long Shot: A scene taken by a camera that has moved back to capture many people or a broad view of the scenery.

Panning: Pivoting or rotating a camera so that it can follow the action in a program. A pan follows the action without the camera having to be moved from its position.

POV: Point of view. The scene as viewed through the eyes of a character. For example, rather than show a character walking down a hallway in a haunted house, the camera shows the nooks, crannies, and shadows that the character would see as he or she walks.

Split Screen: Two different pictures or scenes are shown on the screen at the same time, often side by side.

Super: Short for *superimposition*. One image (words or picture) is shown over another image, as when the title of a show appears over a scene from the show.

Tilting: Changing the angle of a camera up or down.

Zoom: The action or movement of a special type of camera lens. The lens moves from one position (maybe a wide angle) to another (probably a narrow angle or close-up) in one smooth movement. Before the use of zoom lenses, the entire camera had to be moved back and forth.

Developing the Writing

As you read the following short story, think about how you could rewrite it as a TV script.

The Dinner Party
Mona Gardner

The country is India. A colonial official and his wife are giving a large dinner party. They are seated with their guests — army officers and government attachés and their wives, and a visiting American naturalist — in their spacious dining room, which has a bare marble floor, open rafters, and wide glass doors opening onto a veranda.

A spirited discussion springs up between a young girl who insists that women have outgrown the jumping-on-a-chair-at-the-sight-of-a-mouse era and a colonel who says that they haven't.

"A woman's unfailing reaction in any crisis," the colonel says, "is to scream. And while a man may feel like it, he has that ounce more of nerve control than a woman has. And that last ounce is what counts."

The American does not join in the argument but watches the other guests. As he looks, he sees a stange expression come over the face of the hostess. She is staring straight ahead, her muscles contracting slightly. With a slight gesture she summons the native boy standing behind her chair and whispers to him. The boy's eyes widen, and he quickly leaves the room.

Of the guests, none except the American notices this or sees the boy place a bowl of milk on the veranda just outside the open doors.

The American comes to with a start. In India, milk in a bowl means only one thing — bait for a snake. He realizes there must be a cobra in the room. He looks up at the rafters — the likeliest place — but they are bare. Three corners of the room are empty and in the fourth the servants are waiting to serve the next course. There is only one place left — under the table.

His first impulse is to jump back and warn the others, but he knows the commotion would frighten the cobra into striking. He speaks quickly, the tone of his voice so arresting that it sobers everyone.

"I want to know just what control everyone at this table has. I will count three hundred — that's five minutes — and not one of you is to move a muscle. Those who move will forfeit fifty rupees. Ready!"

The twenty people sit like stone images while he counts. He is saying ". . . two hundred and eighty . . ." when, out of the corner of his eye, he sees the cobra emerge and make for the bowl of milk. Screams ring out as he jumps to slam the veranda doors safely shut.

"You were right, Colonel!" the host exclaims. "A man has just shown us an example of perfect control."

"Just a minute," the American says, turning to his hostess. "Mrs. Wynnes, how did you know that cobra was in the room?"

A faint smile lights up the woman's face as she replies: "Because it was crawling across my foot."

With a small group, prepare a short television script for all or part of this story. You could divide the story up with other groups in the class so that each prepares a different part of the script. For example, who will do the introduction? Who will set the scene? Who will complete the story?

Once your group has decided exactly what it is going to script, you will need to consider questions such as these:

1. How many characters will appear?
2. How will the setting be shown?
3. What properties, costumes, and lighting will be needed?
4. What will the various characters say?
5. Will there be a narrator?

Review the television terms given in the Preparing to Write section. You will have to decide, for instance, when you'd like to show a close-up, an establishing shot, a head shot, a fade out, and so on.

After you have done some preliminary planning, go ahead and write your script.

Revising and Editing

Ask an audience who has not read the original story that you began with to read both that story and your television script. Ask them to note similarities and differences between the two versions. Use their comments to help you edit your script.

Sharing and Publishing

As a class, choose one or more of the scripts to act out. If you have film-making equipment, you could turn them into films. Share your work with another class in the school.

Growing from Writing

A. It is necessary for television commercials to be carefully scripted.

Prepare a script for a one-minute television commercial advertising a food product. Your commercial has only one character — the narrator. The narrator can be given a role; for example, a parent, a cook, a waiter.

You will have to decide when you want to show the narrator, when you want to show the product, when you want to show a long shot of the whole scene, and so on. Include camera directions in your script.

B. Examine a page from a television guide and choose a show that you might be interested in watching.

Prepare a television script based on the TV guide's brief summary of this television program. Script only one scene from the program, using only a few characters and not more than one setting.

Adventure in the Air

Adventure stories almost always involve exciting conflict. Forces — human, natural, and/or supernatural — struggle against each other. It is conflict that creates tension and excitement in a story. It makes the reader want to continue reading, in order to find out how the conflict is resolved.

Somebody Fell From Aloft
Retold by ALVIN SCHWARTZ

I had signed on as an ordinary seaman on the *Falls of Ettrick,* a merchant ship bound for England. The first time I saw that ship, I knew her right away. She was the old *Gertrude Spurshoe.* I had sailed on her years before when she was painted brown and gold. Now she was painted black and had a new name, but it was the same ship for sure.

We had a pretty good crew for that voyage, except for one hard-looking ticket named McLaren. He was a pretty good seaman, but there was something about him that I didn't trust. He was kind of secretive. Kept mostly to himself.

One day somebody told him that I had worked on the old *Gertrude.* For some reason he got all a-tremble over that. Then I ketched him giving me all of these ugly black looks, as if he was itchin' to knife me in the back. I guessed it had something to do with the *Gertrude,* but I didn't know what.

Well, this one day we was tryin' to work our way through a drippin' black fog. You'd scarcely know we had all the lights on. And it was dead calm. There wasn't a breath of fresh air.

The ship just lay there wallowing in a trough, a-rollin' and a-rollin', goin' nowheres.

I was standing my watch around midships, and McLaren was doin' his trick at the wheel. The rest of the crew was scattered around one place and another. It was as quiet as could be.

Then all at once — WHACKO! This thing hits the deck right in front of McLaren! He lets go a screech that turns my blood cold and he falls down in a faint.

The second mate starts yellin' that somebody has fallen from aloft. Layin' out there just forward of the wheel was someone, or something, dressed in oilskins with blood oozin' out from underneath. The captain ran and fetched a big light from his cabin so we could see who it was.

They kind of straightened him out to get a good look at his face. He was a big, ugly-lookin' devil. But nobody knew who he was or what he was doin' up there. At least nobody was sayin'.

When McLaren came to from his faint, they tried to get somethin' out of him. All he did was jabber away and keep rollin' those big, wild-looking eyes of his.

Everybody was gettin' more and more excited. We all wanted to heave the body overboard as quick as we could. There was somethin' weird about it, as if it wasn't real.

But the captain wasn't so sure about getting rid of it that way. "Could it be a stowaway?" he asked. But the ship was so filled with lumber we were carryin', there was no space where a livin' thing could hide for three weeks, which is how long we had been out. Even if it was a stowaway, what was it doing aloft on such a dirty day? There was no reason for anyone to be up there. There was nothin' to see.

Finally, the captain gave up and told us to heave him overboard. Then nobody would touch him. The mate ordered us to pick him up, but nobody made a move. Then he tried coaxin', but that didn't do any good.

Suddenly that loony McLaren starts yellin', "I handled him once, and I can handle him again!" He picks up the body, and staggers over to the railin' with it. He is just about to throw it overboard when it wraps its two big, long arms around him, and over they go together! Then on the way down, one of them starts laughin' in a horrible way.

The mates are yellin' to launch a boat, but nobody would get into a boat, not on a night like that. We threw a couple of life preservers after them, but everybody knew they wouldn't help. So that was that. Or was it?

The first chance I had to go home after that, I went right over to see old Captain Spurshoe, who was captain when the *Gertrude* was around.

"Well," he says, "one trip these two outlandish men shipped aboard the *Gertrude*. One was McLaren, the other was a really big fella. The big one was always pickin' on McLaren and thumpin' him around. And McLaren was always talkin' about how he would get back at him.

"Well, this wet, dirty night the two of them was up there alone, and the big one come flyin' down, killed himself deader'n a herring.

"McLaren says the foot rope they were using parted and how he almost fell himself. But everybody who saw that rope knew she didn't give away on her own. She had been cut through with a knife.

"After that whenever we came into port, McLaren thought we were goin' to get the police after him, and he'd get pretty scared. But we couldn't prove anything, so we didn't try. In the end, I guess the big fella took care of things in his own way. If he was a ghost that came back, that's what he was — if there be things like ghosts."

BUILDING A WRITING CONTEXT

1. **How does the writer's style help make the story strong?**
2. **How does the author create interest in McLaren near the beginning of the story?**
3. **What is the main conflict in the story?**
4. **What questions does the author seem to have left unanswered? Why?**

THE WRITING WORKSHOP

Preparing to Write

When you write an adventure story, you can feel as if you are *in* the adventure. You can live through your most exciting and nerve-tingling fantasies, as you identify with the experiences of your characters.

As you explore this writing assignment, let yourself take risks and grapple head-on with opposing forces. A great deal of satisfaction can come from the act of creating your own adventure story.

Developing the Writing

In planning your story, you will need to decide what type of conflict you will have; for example:
- A person fighting nature.
- A person encountering the supernatural.
- A person (or group) in conflict with another person or group.
- A person attempting to discover a special place or an object of great importance.

Choose one of the following situations, or invent a situation of your own. Either alone or in a small group, use the situation to write a short adventure story. You are writing this story to share with your classmates.

A. You are chasing, or being chased, in your neighbourhood. You and your enemy are both on foot. Describe how you would use your neighbourhood to hide from or overtake him or her. You might even walk around your neighborhood before you begin the story, noting a few places that seem good for hiding. You might include street names and house numbers in your description so that, when the story is read aloud, others in the class can get a clearer picture of what you are describing.

B. A small colony of people — led by a scientist with only one eye — lives its own life, separate from the rest of society. The colony is very well organized. It supports itself by farming and by making and selling flying saucer models. Two outsiders who have visited the colony have disappeared without a trace. One dark night, while travelling alone, you accidentally wander into the colony. What happens?

C. You are shipwrecked on a desert island. You try to flag down passing ships, but nobody notices your signals. At last, on the fourth day, a ship approaches your island. You notice her name on the hull: *The Codseeker*. A shiver runs down your spine. You know that *The Codseeker* sank in these waters 300 years ago. The captain, dressed in old-fashioned clothes, waves to you from the deck. He throws you a rope. What do you do?

D. You thought you knew all about the apartment building where you live. However, one day while returning from the swimming pool in the basement, you discover a secret passageway. It's behind an almost invisible sliding door, made to look like part of the wall. You decide to explore. Where does the passageway lead? What happens to you?

Revising and Editing

A. Take another look at your opening sentences. Do they help the reader to become involved in your story immediately?

Exchange stories with a classmate who wrote on the same topic. Compare your opening sentences. What can you learn from each other? How could you both improve your openings? Do it.

B. Reread your whole story.
- Is it possible to improve some sentences by inserting additional words (or phrases) anywhere within them?
- Can you improve your writing by omitting some of the original words?
- Can some sentences be improved by keeping the original words but rearranging their order?

Make any changes you think will improve your story.

Sharing and Publishing

Share your story with your classmates, either by reading it aloud or adding it to a bulletin board or wall display.

Growing from Writing

A. Choose a natural disaster, such as a volcanic eruption, earthquake, or flood. Build an episode of an adventure tale around this disaster. By using researched information concerning your natural disaster, you can give your story a realistic feeling.

B. You are driving home and a great snowstorm begins to rage. You are worried. Everything around you is white and confusing. You can barely see where you are going. Suddenly your car stalls. You are far from home and don't really know where you are. Now you can't see a thing. What do you do? Do you stay in your car or leave it? How do you keep alive and warm? Do you have a special reason for wanting to get home? Write an adventure story based on this situation.

Legends

The Magic Buffalo

Myths and legends are stories that have come down to us from the distant past. As you will discover, most are exciting tales of adventure, often including magic. Many are stories of the struggle between good and evil.

Most legends were told by storytellers long before they were written down. And they were told with a purpose. Myths are often about gods and goddesses and super-human beings. They were generally told to explain a belief or something in nature. Legends are almost always based on something that actually happened. They were told to glorify someone who had performed great deeds or caused marvellous things to happen.

Buffalo Lake   Retold by ELLA ELIZABETH CLARK

Buffalo Lake is located in Alberta, southeast of Edmonton and not far from Red Deer Lake.

This tradition of the Sarcee Indians was told in 1954 by Daisy Otter. The Blackfoot of Montana relate almost the same story about Buffalo Lake. The second part of the story is similar to one that the Kootenays tell about Flathead Lake, Montana, and to one that the Nez Perce Indians tell about Snake River in Idaho.

In the early days the Sarcee tribe was big. One fall when they were in the Red Deer country, two young men went out to hunt buffalo. Quite a long distance from their camp they saw a buffalo bull standing in a dry valley.

"How can we get a close shot at him?" one young man asked the other.

"Let's chase him," answered the other. "We cannot reach him from here with our bows and arrows."

So they chased the buffalo bull and killed him. Then they began to butcher him, to get the skin and the meat.

"You cut his legs off," one hunter said, "and I will cut him open."

So the man cut off the front legs and one of the hind legs, while the other cut the buffalo open. As he finished, water began to come out of the body, just as a running spring comes out of the side of a mountain.

The men stopped their work and watched. When they saw that the stream continued to flow, they went up on a hill and sat there to watch it. Soon water covered the buffalo's body. Then it began to fill up the little hollow place where the animal had fallen when they killed it. Soon it formed a pool in the shape of a buffalo. A little stream ran out from the place that looked like the tail.

The men watched from the hill until evening. By that time the water had become a large lake, still in the shape of a buffalo. Some willow trees which had been there for a long time now stood beside the part that looked like a head. So the buffalo-shaped lake seemed to have hair.

Late in the evening the hunters returned to camp and told their people about the strange happening and the new lake. Next morning, very early, all the people went with the two men, to see the sight. Sure enough, there was a big lake, in the shape of a buffalo. A stream ran from its tail; and at the spine, where the water was very deep, the animal was deep blue.

Then the people moved on farther north to continue the buffalo hunt. When winter came and it was time to go south again, the head man of the tribe learned that the new lake was frozen over.

"Let's travel south over the new lake," he said to his people. "We can save time by going across it instead of around it."

So they packed their things on horses and on travois and started across the lake. When some of them had crossed to the opposite side, and some were on the lake, a little boy saw a bone sticking out of the ice.

"I would like to have that bone," he said to his grandmother, who was walking with him. "Will you get it for me?"

"It is the horn of a buffalo," said his grandmother.

She took her axe and began pounding the horn with it, trying to break it off.

All the people near her stopped their horses and their dogs to watch the grandmother. She pounded and pounded, there where the horn touched the ice. Suddenly a big cracking noise startled everyone, as the ice split wide open. Indians, horses, dogs — all that were on the lake fell in and were drowned. Only the people on the shores, those who had crossed over and those who had not yet started, were saved, from all that band of Sarcees.

That is how the Sarcees got divided. Those in the north became known as Beaver and Chipewyan. Those in the south kept the name of Sarcee. The Beaver Indians speak the same language, except that they talk faster than the Sarcees do.

When you pass Buffalo Lake in the evening, you can hear dogs barking and children playing and shouting down in the bottom of the lake. They are the ones that fell through the ice, long, long ago.

BUILDING A WRITING CONTEXT

1. **This legend tells of the division of the Sarcee Indian people into two groups: the Beaver and Chipewyan group, and the Sarcee group. Often a legend begins from a true experience, but as it is told over and over, it gains aspects of mysticism, magic, and superstition. What mystical aspects exist in the story? How do you think this legend began?**
2. **How is geography important to this story?**

THE WRITING WORKSHOP

Preparing to Write

A legend is a tradition or story handed down from earlier times and popularly accepted as at least partly true. *Legend* originally meant a story about a saint, but the word is now applied to any partly fictitious tale concerning a real person, event, or place. A legend is likely to be less concerned with the supernatural than a myth, but *legend* and *myth* are related terms.

Developing the Writing

A. The name Buffalo Lake is quite unique, and it leads naturally to imaginative thoughts as to its origin. List 10 interesting place names found in your province or territory. Select one of these and write a legend telling how the name began.

B. As progress pushes against unexplored frontiers, making them ever smaller, it is becoming more and more difficult to find unexplored areas in the world. The following areas, however, are still relatively unexplored. Research one of these areas and create a legend about it.
  1. Northern Alaska's great Brooks Range.
  2. The Amazon River basin.
  3. Antarctica.
  4. The Canadian Arctic.
  5. Greenland.
  6. The Guiana Highlands (South America).
  7. The Himalayan Mountain Range (Asia).
  8. Micronesia (consisting of the Mariana, Marshall, Caroline, and Gilbert island groups, located east of the Philippines).
  9. New Guinea.
10. Rub al Khali (a part of the Arabian Desert).

C. Write a story about some strange, unusual, or unreal event in such detail as to make it seem real, vivid, and believable to the reader. Suggested subjects: seeing a ghost; being arrested and held in jail in a case of mistaken identity; being bitten by a rattlesnake while alone in the desert; discovering that you've had a previous life.

Revising and Editing

After you've written your story, edit it using the following questions:
- Have I used the appearance of the character(s) to tell my readers what kinds of people they are?
- Have I used dialogue to reveal the nature of the character(s)?
- Have I used the characters' actions to reveal the kinds of people they are?
- Have I really created or recreated an event, rather than just telling *about* it?
- Have I made the event seem real to the reader?

Sharing and Publishing

If possible, read your story aloud to a group of students, perhaps a younger class in your school.

Growing from Writing

A. Put yourself in the role of a person who lived in an earlier era. Have him or her visit our society today. What would this person think about modern-day Canada? Present this as a dramatic monologue to your classmates.

B. The origin of words is quite diverse, sometimes coming from legend, sometimes from fact. The following people's names became words that are often used in our language. Research five of the people's lives, determining what words came from their names. Write a brief explanation for each of the five that you research.
1. Amelia Jenks Bloomer (1818-1894)
2. Thomas Bowdler (1745-1825)
3. Capt. Charles C. Boycott (1832-1897)
4. Louis Braille (1809-1852)
5. Rudolf Diesel (1858-1913)
6. Joseph I. Guillotin (1738-1814)
7. Charles Lynch (1736-1796)
8. John Montagu (1718-1792)
9. Jean Nicot (1530?-1600)
10. Maj. Vidkun Quisling (1887-1945)
11. Antoine Joseph Sax (1814-1894)
12. Étienne de Silhouette (1709-1767)

Tales

The Sundance Kid in Alberta

Author Andy Russell was born in 1915 and raised on a ranch near the foothills of Alberta. He left high school during the Depression of the 1930s, and has been a successful trapper, bronco-buster, mountain guide, cattle-rancher, writer, and photographer. In 1977 he received the Order of Canada.

In Russell's boyhood, the foothills of the Rockies were still frontier country, and horses were the only kind of transportation. Around the evening fires, Russell heard stories told by people who had known the country when it was all open range. These stories were filled with action, adventure, and humour, and probably held a flavour of nostalgia. As a boy, Russell learned the tricks of riding and roping, and how to handle guns. He grew up with an interest in the history of the cowboy and the west. Here is just one of the many stories that he heard and later recorded in writing.

from *Men of the Saddle*
TED GRANT and ANDY RUSSELL

In 1890 Harry Longbaugh, a quiet handsome young man, showed up at the Bar U ranch near High River looking for a job. He was an excellent rider and had no trouble getting work with Herb Millar, who was breaking horses for the ranch at that time. Nobody knew that back in Wyoming he was known as the Sundance Kid. . . .

At the annual roundups, Longbaugh was rated a top hand and was a popular cowboy. Nobody knew that he was also one of the fastest and deadliest gunmen ever to show up in western Canada. He stayed around for two or three years and was respected as a good hand and a law-abiding man.

But then one winter he went into partnership with Frank Hamilton, a bully who owned a bar in Calgary. On several previous occasions Hamilton had taken partners to do most of the work; then when it had come time to split the earnings, he had picked a quarrel and beat them up, thrown them out, and kept the money. He tried it with Harry Longbaugh to his sorrow.

Harry was behind the bar when the row started. Moving with the grace and power of a cougar, he placed his left hand on top of the bar and vaulted over it in a twisting jump. When his boots hit the floor, a .45 six-shooter had appeared as if by magic in his other hand and it was jammed into Hamilton's middle. The money was not long in changing hands. The cowboy backed out of the place, got his horse, and promptly disappeared.

He headed south into Montana, where he contacted some old friends, Butch Cassidy and Kid Curry. They set out on a ten-year long trail of holding up banks and trains all through the western States. Finally, hard pressed by the law, they quit the country, heading for South America, where they proceeded to raise hell in a similar fashion. Eventually they were cornered by a contingent of Bolivian cavalry and went under in a blaze of gunfire.

BUILDING A WRITING CONTEXT

1. **What might account for Harry Longbaugh's quiet respectable behaviour when he arrived in High River, compared with his behaviour later?**
2. **Outlaws like Jesse James, Cole Younger, Butch Cassidy, and the Sundance Kid have often been considered folk heroes. Should this be the case in your opinion? Explain.**

THE WRITING WORKSHOP

Preparing to Write

How does the tale from *Men of the Saddle* fit the following guidelines for the writing of this type of narration?
- Characters should be introduced in an interesting and/or dramatic way.
- The tale should show a clear plan of procedure.
- The events of the tale should be told in the order in which they happened.
- The tale should centre on, or at least include, some major conflict.

Developing the Writing

Keep the above guidelines in mind as you carry out one or both of the following writing assignments.

A. No dialogue is included in the tale from *Men of the Saddle*. Rewrite all or part of it, including appropriate dialogue.

B. A number of dramatic incidents and characters have contributed to the legends of the North American west. Research one of the following. Choose an incident that you discover in your research and retell it in the form of a tale to present to your classmates. Include dialogue in your tale.
1. Butch Cassidy's Wild Bunch (western United States and South America).
2. Matthew Baillie Begbie, the "Hanging Judge" (British Columbia).
3. Almighty Voice (Duck Lake, Saskatchewan).
4. Major Sam Steele (western Canada).
5. The epic showdown at the O.K. Corral (Tombstone, Arizona).
6. The James gang (central United States).
7. Morris "Two-Gun" Cohen (Edmonton, Alberta).
8. The Mad Trapper of Rat River (Canadian North).

Revising and Editing

A. Reread your tale, editing it as necessary according to the guidelines given in the Preparing to Write section.

B. Dialogue in a story should make the characters come alive. Reread your tale once more, editing the dialogue as necessary according to the following guidelines.
- Make sure it is clear who is speaking and who is being spoken to. Identify the speaker if it is not clear from context.
- Use dialogue tags to indicate the speaker's tone of voice. Examples of dialogue tags: *he said harshly*, and *she replied, spitting out the words.* However, don't overdo the use of dialogue tags.
- Avoid long speeches. Break up long speeches by having a give-and-take between characters.
- Try to catch the patterns of conversational speech in your written dialogue — slang, incomplete sentences, and so on.

Sharing and Publishing

Present your tale to your classmates, either by putting it up on a bulletin board or wall for them to read, or by reading it aloud.

Growing from Writing

A. If possible, view the National Film Board film "The Days of Whiskey Gap." It deals with the condition of law and order in Alberta during the late 1800s (the time of Harry Longbaugh).

B. Research the early history of the North West Mounted Police. In what important ways did they make the history of the Canadian west different from that of the American west? Write a brief report and share it with your classmates.

Paragraphs

Bird's Eye View

Usually a *paragraph* is a group of sentences about one event or idea. This event or idea is called the *topic*. There are several different kinds of paragraphs. Those that basically describe or paint a picture of a particular person, place, thing, or event are known as *descriptive paragraphs*. Paragraphs that mainly tell a story are *narrative paragraphs*. Paragraphs that tell how to do something or that explain something are *expository paragraphs*.

Very few paragraphs have only one purpose. Most are a combination of two or three types. For instance, a paragraph that tells a story may do so in a fairly descriptive way.

from Two Against the North FARLEY MOWAT

As the sunlight fell upon it Jamie's eyes grew wide with wonder, for in his hand he held a sword! And what a sword it was. Four feet (1.2 m) in length, it had a double-edged blade and a two-handed hilt. It was the sort of weapon that only a giant of a man could have handled. The blade was deeply pitted and rusted and on the hilt were broad rings of gold, turned greenish by centuries of weather.

from The Pigman PAUL ZINDEL

As I started moving away and heading for the door John went to Mr. Pignati and just took his arm lightly, trying to turn him away from the empty cage. I saw the Pigman open his mouth, and then his hands started to shake. He went to grab hold of the railing, but let out a tiny cry almost like a puppy that had been stepped on by mistake. I can still remember the sound of it, and sometimes I wake up from a nightmare with it in my ears. It was like a high-pitched scream, but it came from deep inside of him, and before John or I knew what had happened, the Pigman dropped to the floor. It seemed as if the monkeys knew something had happened because they started making noise and pulling against the bars. I thought they were going to tear them out of the frames, and I wanted to put my hands to my ears to shut out the jungle that had surrounded us.

Mr. Pignati was dead.

from Wormlore BETTY ROOTS

You have probably seen a bird standing on a lawn turning its head from side to side. Some people think this shows that birds listen for worms. But you have only to let a worm crawl over a wet piece of paper to know that this is very unlikely. (Bristles do not rustle on wet paper — nor do they on soil.) No, the bird is peering down the burrows of worms, first with one eye and then with the other. Worms have a habit of staying near the surface and can be seen by the sharp eyes of birds.

BUILDING A WRITING CONTEXT

1. **Which of the above paragraphs is mainly descriptive? Mainly narrative? Mainly expository?**
2. **In what ways is the descriptive paragraph different from the narrative paragraph?**
3. **What is the topic of each paragraph?**

THE WRITING WORKSHOP

Preparing to Write
Study the chart.

THE PARAGRAPH AND ITS PARTS

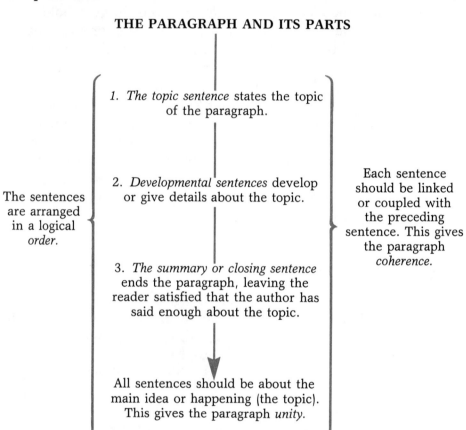

The sentences are arranged in a logical order.

1. *The topic sentence* states the topic of the paragraph.

2. *Developmental sentences* develop or give details about the topic.

3. *The summary or closing sentence* ends the paragraph, leaving the reader satisfied that the author has said enough about the topic.

Each sentence should be linked or coupled with the preceding sentence. This gives the paragraph *coherence.*

All sentences should be about the main idea or happening (the topic). This gives the paragraph *unity.*

Sentence variety is achieved by varying the length and kinds of sentences, and the order of the parts within sentences.

Developing the Writing
A. Descriptive Paragraph
Select a topic with which you are very familiar. A family member, your room, your pet, a favourite dress, or a favourite place are possibilities.

Brainstorm a thought web to get you started. Example:

Wildlife.
- Perch, sunfish, a family of ducks.
- A fast furry martin.
- A chorus of small birds.

Water.
- Warm.
- Clear.
- Smooth as glass.

My secret swimming hole.

Sunning rock.
- Flat, grey-green.
- Smooth.
- A natural ramp connecting the forest to the pool.

Trees.
- Dense.
- Green, lush.
- Like a privacy fence.

Rope swing.
- Brown, thick.
- Warm, frayed.
- Hangs from the maple tree.
- Swings me Tarzan-like over the water.

Decide on your topic statement. Use the chart to ensure that you include all the elements of a basic paragraph in your description.

B. Narrative Paragraph

To write a narrative paragraph, you need to focus on what happened and tell it step by step. Your reader should be able to see the events unfold in his or her mind. Use strong verbs when writing narrative paragraphs, and present the events in a logical order.

Select a topic you know very well — something that actually happened to you, or that you witnessed.

In your notebook complete the writing plan below:

Topic: _____

_____

Ideas for an opening sentence: _____

_____

Ideas for developmental sentences: _____

_____

_____

Ideas for a closing sentence: _____

_____

Now write your narrative paragraph.

C. **Expository Paragraph**

In an expository paragraph you explain ideas or outline how to do something. Be careful to include all necessary details, to present them in the proper order, and to give directions clearly.

For your topic select something you know well. Examples:
- How I clean my room.
- How to care for my pet
- How to play . . .
- How to make . . .

In your notebook complete the writing plan below:

Topic: _____

_____

Ideas for an opening sentence: _____

_____

Ideas for developmental sentences: _____

_____

_____

_____

_____

Ideas for a closing sentence: _____

_____

Now write your expository paragraph.

Revising and Editing

In groups of three take turns reading your paragraphs aloud.
Listen to all the descriptive paragraphs first, and then discuss
their strong and weak points. Do the same for the narrative and
expository paragraphs. Use the following questions as a guide in
evaluating and improving your paragraphs.

1. Does the paragraph have an effective opening, middle, and
   ending?
2. Does it have coherence; that is, does it "hold together" well?
3. Are details listed in a logical order?
4. Have time words such as *first* and *next* been used well?
5. Should any details be added to make the explanation more
   complete?
6. Are there ideas, words, etc. that don't seem to have a real
   purpose, or that are uninteresting or confusing? Should these
   be removed?
7. Should any sentences, words, or phrases be reordered to
   make the paragraph clearer?

Sharing and Publishing

Organize some of your expository paragraphs into a class book
with a title such as *How-To's from Our Class*.

Growing from Writing

A. Select three novels by different authors and compare how
they use narrative paragraphs. Share your information with a
partner who has done the same thing.

B. Reproduce your descriptive paragraph in another form. You
could do it in the form of a picture, diagram, or clay model.

Journals

Simon Meets the Fraser

In 1805 Simon Fraser was appointed to explore and establish trading posts in the Canadian Rockies for the North West Company. He led a party of trappers and traders from Alberta's Peace River district into British Columbia. Beyond the Rocky Mountains he came upon the river now called the Fraser (but thought by Simon Fraser to be the Columbia).

In 1808, after spending three years exploring British Columbia and establishing trading posts, Fraser decided to canoe down the river he had found. Native people told him it was impossible because of the many rapids, and they were right. The banks were so steep that the explorers could not even portage their canoes, and had to abandon them. Undeterred, Fraser led them on foot to where the river becomes navigable again. After bargaining with friendly Native people for new canoes, they paddled south, only to be stopped again by rapids and canyons.

After another 100 miles (about 160 km) the river turned west and became navigable. In a few days Fraser reached tidewater near modern-day Vancouver. Knowing the mouth of the Columbia was much farther south, Fraser finally realized he was not on that river. Instead he had explored a previously little-known waterway — the wild river that, fittingly enough, was later named the Fraser.

Following is an excerpt from the journal Fraser kept while on his voyage. Also included is a recorded reaction from a Native storyteller.

Journal of a Voyage from the Rocky Mountain to the Pacific Performed in the Year 1808 SIMON FRASER

Thursday, June 15, 1808: Here we are, in a strange country; surrounded with dangers and difficulties; among numberless tribes of savages, who never saw the face of a white man: however we shall endeavour to make the best of it. Some of the Indians who had joined us had joined us yesterday forenoon, who we were happy to acknowledge now as old acquaintance, drew at my request a chart of the country below this to the sea. By this sketch the navigation seems still very bad, and difficult. At some distance to the east appears another large river which runs parallel to this to the sea. After obtaining the information required we prevailed upon the Indians to ferry us over to the village. Having employed but one canoe which made three trips, they took up considerable time in this passage. The village is a fortification 100 by 24 feet (about 30 m by 7 m); surrounded with palisades 18 feet (about 5 m) high, slanting inwards, and lined with a shorter row that supports a shade covered with bark, which constitute the dwellings. This is the metropolis of the Askettih (Lillooet) Nation.

How the Lillooets Saw Simon Fraser

From The British Columbia Indian Language Project, a recording of Lillooet Indian storyteller Sam Mitchell.

This is a story about some people who came down the Fraser River a long time ago. A man named "Piyell" used to tell my father about this. These "drifters," as they were called, stopped at the "Drop-off Spot" on the river, where the rapids are, below the Bridge River Village. These "drifters" landed their boat, and saw some Indians there. They asked these Indians to help them carry their boat around this rough water area.

The man who told this story to my father was only a baby when this happened; he was only two years old. The leader of these "drifters" (a white man) had a tattoo of the sun on his forehead, and a tatoo of the moon on his chest. They put the boat back in the water, below the rapids, and carried on toward

Lillooet. There were some Indians there who wanted to go after these white men and steal all their possessions, but the leader told them, "Don't bother them — they might be able to help us one day."

Many times this story was told to me. Recently, I was told by the whites that this person who came down the river was called "Simon Fraser," and that this happened in the year 1808.

BUILDING A WRITING CONTEXT

1. **On a map of British Columbia, trace the Fraser River from its beginnings on the west slope of the Rocky Mountains, down to the Pacific Ocean. List the names of five modern-day communities along the river.**
2. **Why do you think most early Canadian explorers kept journals? What might have happened if they hadn't?**

THE WRITING WORKSHOP

Preparing to Write

Most people write notes to themselves. But often they lose these notes, especially if they are written on torn bits of paper, the backs of grocery lists, or the flyleaves of books. A pleasant alternative to this type of random note-keeping is a journal — a bound ruled book in which to make instant and permanent entries. Many professional writers keep journals.

A journal is a record, an entry-book — kept regularly, though not necessarily daily. It is a record kept for oneself. As such, it may be fragmentary, allusive, disjointed, and uneven in quality. It is not meant to be polished and coherent. If it were, then it would be a collection of essays.

A journal entry is not only a record *for* oneself, but also *of* oneself. Every memorable journal, any successful journal, is honest. A journal may be many things:

1. Think of your journal as a treasury for quotes (others' and/or your own), ideas, insights, puns, impressions, mental images.
2. Think of your journal as a storehouse into which you pack goods for a rainy day, when you can browse through with delight and nostalgia and amazement.

3. Think of your journal as a laboratory for experiments —
   blank pages waiting to be tried. Ask questions, and set about
   finding answers.
4. Think of your journal as a tape-recorder attached directly to
   your brain. Sometimes you can simply record your stream-of-
   consciousness thoughts. Don't fuss about exact words: simply
   write them as fast as you think. You can polish your writing
   later if you wish.
5. Think of your journal as a letter to yourself. What would you
   have yourself know? Or what would you like to remember
   ten years from now? Which self of your many selves will you
   choose to write to?

Developing the Writing

A. Try keeping a journal for a week. You may think you are
not the journal kind of person — maybe you have a
photographic memory or an aversion to recording anything you
feel has not been polished like a gem. But try keeping a journal
for a week anyway, and see what happens.

B. Find a paragraph or short passage you admire. Copy it into
your journal. Take brief notes on what it says. The next day
attempt to reproduce the passage without looking at it. Compare
the two versions. In what ways do you prefer the original? In
what ways do you prefer your own version?

C. Choose one of the following topics, or make up a similar
topic of your own. For a week, note in your journal all the
examples you can find that fit your topic.
1. Ways people waste time.
2. Embarrassing situations.
3. Ways people try to improve themselves.
4. Interesting gestures people use as they talk.

D. The insights and observations of people who have delighted
in, and been fascinated by, the wonders of the natural
environment are a source of inspiration for many people. A
number of writers (for example, Roderick Haig-Brown) have
captured their insights in words and offered them to others.

Sit quietly in an outdoor setting. Listen carefully for the sounds
of nature, and look at your surroundings. At first, try not to

focus on any one thing, but on the whole landscape at once. Then look at specific things, such as a bird flying or an insect on the ground.

Write in your journal, in any style, about your experience.

Revising and Editing

After keeping a journal for a week, stop for a week. Then go back to your journal. Choose the entry that most moves you, and work it up or cut it down until you have produced a piece of writing that is satisfying to you.

Growing from Writing

A. Undertake an extended observation project in which you record impressions on one of the following topics in your journal for about two weeks.
1. Ethnic influences in your community.
2. Connections between the people in your community and the world beyond.
3. People who have unique skills or talents.
4. Ways your community is deteriorating and ways it is improving.

B. For the next two weeks, select one of the following topics per day, and discuss it in a journal entry.
1. Growing pains.
2. My life and hard times.
3. My experience in hospitals.
4. Kindergarten as I remember it.
5. It shouldn't have happened to a dog.
6. The person who hesitates is lost.
7. My conscience is my guide.
8. My ambitions.
9. A strong influence in my life.
10. I learn from experience.
11. My problem.
12. The house I remember best.
13. The best class period so far this term.
14. I kept my resolution.
15. An important decision.
16. The world I left behind.

17. An unusual incident.
18. I was there.
19. A day I would like to forget.
20. Too far from home.
21. A tense moment.
22. Clouds in the sky.
23. I was a hero.
24. If I could do it over.
25. Too early in the morning.
26. Champion!
27. A boaster deflated.
28. In one ear.
29. I knew it would happen.
30. A motto to live by.

Reminiscences

Let's Go Fly a Kite

Author Benjamin Franklin (1706-1790) was a famous American statesman, scientist, and inventor. Growing up in Boston, a seaport surrounded by water, Franklin learned early to swim well and to manage boats.

In a letter written in 1773, Franklin recalled some of his early swimming and boating experiments, which foreshadowed his later work as a scientist and inventor. This letter was written in 1773 about an event that had taken place some 60 years earlier.

One Way to Cross a Pond
BENJAMIN FRANKLIN

When I was a boy, I amused myself one day with flying a paper kite; and approaching the bank of a pond, which was near a mile (1.6 km) broad, I tied the string to a stake, and the kite ascended to a very considerable height above the pond, while I was swimming.

In a little time, being desirous of amusing myself with my kite, and enjoying at the same time the pleasure of swimming, I returned, and loosing from the stake the string with the little stick which was fastened to it, went again into the water, where I found that lying on my back and holding the stick in my hands, I was drawn along the surface of the water in a very agreeable manner. Having then engaged another boy to carry my clothes round the pond to a place which I pointed out to him on the other side, I began to cross the pond with my kite, which carried me quite over without the least fatigue, and with the greatest pleasure imaginable.

I was only obliged occasionally to halt a little in my course and resist its progress when it appeared that, by following too quickly, I lowered the kite too much, by doing which occasionally I made it rise again.

I have never since that time practised this singular mode of swimming, though I think it not impossible to cross in this manner from Dover to Calais. The ferry, however, is still preferable.

BUILDING A WRITING CONTEXT

1. **What kind of person do you think Franklin was as a boy? List at least five words and phrases to describe him.**
2. **Make a simple sketch illustrating Franklin's boyhood experiment as described in this excerpt.**

THE WRITING WORKSHOP

Preparing to Write

Remembering childhood is not childish, but wise and necessary. We think back on our childhood because we loved those years of play. We go back to our childhood because in writing about those years we, in a sense, gain a second life.

Many of the best writers have taken journeys into their pasts, exploring their childhood years in their writing. As a junior high school student, you are in a good position to write about your childhood. Some people say that writers require about seven years' distance between themselves and the events recalled, in order to write them from a really effective perspective.

If you write of yesterday's or last year's events, you usually remember them so well that you may leave them shrouded in your nearby intimate memories, which the reader does not share. If several years have gone by, you are able to "step outside" the memory and see it more in the way your readers will.

50

Developing the Writing

A. Choose from your childhood an experience you can't forget. Write it down in story form. The following suggested topics may give you some ideas.

1. My first fight.
2. My first dollar.
3. My first ten years were the hardest.
4. My most important decision and why I made it.
5. My first encounter with racial discrimination.
6. My most embarrassing moment.
7. The stupidest thing I ever did.
8. My most serious accident.
9. My narrowest escape.
10. The longest minute I ever spent.
11. The wisest thing I ever did.
12. Moving to a strange community.

B. Benjamin Franklin's printing shop in Philadelphia gave him a chance to share his wit and humour with many people. His book *Poor Richard's Almanac* includes the following wise sayings, or proverbs. Choose five and explain them in your own words.

- "Early to bed and early to rise, make a man healthy, wealthy, and wise."
- "Better slip with foot than by tongue."
- "He that doth what he should not, shall feel what he would not."
- "Light purse, heavy heart."
- "Great talkers, little doers."
- "Well done is better than well said."
- "Don't throw stones at your neighbours if your own windows are glass."
- "Look ahead or you will find yourself behind."
- "A cat in gloves catches no mice."
- "God helps them that help themselves."
- "No gains without pains."
- "He that falls in love with himself will have no rivals."
- "The rotten apple spoils his companions."

C. Write a personal-experience story illustrating one of the proverbs in Activity B above. Your story may be either real or made up.

Revising and Editing

Most good published pieces of writing have been created in several drafts — each draft better than the last. What you see in print is almost never the first effort. No professional writer expects to dash off a piece of writing that is beyond improvement. The writer thinks of each draft as preliminary to another better version, until he or she is finally satisfied and says, "Done."

Look at the first draft of one story you wrote in this chapter. Is there some other place on the first page where the story could begin satisfactorily — other than where you began? Look for a spot where the story itself seems to start up, not simply where you began it.

If possible, intrigue the reader with your story beginning. Create tension, suspense, or surprise, or begin an action that carries the reader along, making him or her continually ask: "What next?"

When you have found or created a good beginning to your story, consider its ending. At both ends of a piece of writing, a writer can fall into the trap of explaining too much, almost as if he or she wanted to give advice to the reader on how to read the piece of writing. Instead of explaining, look over your story for a spot near the end that is exciting or surprising, and consider stopping here. Or near the end find a good detail — an example of one of the main feelings or ideas in the story — and try chopping off everything else that follows it. Or move the particularly striking passage to the end position. Try different methods of ending until you find the one that seems best for this particular story.

Growing from Writing

"What are you most afraid of?" a team of market researchers asked 3000 adults. Many named more than one fear. The results may surprise you.

Biggest Fear	% naming
1. Speaking before a group	41
2. Heights	32
3. Insects and bugs	22
4. Financial problems	22

5.	Deep water	22
6.	Sickness	19
7.	Death	19
8.	Flying	18
9.	Loneliness	14
10.	Dogs	11
11.	Driving/riding in a car	9
12.	Darkness	8
13.	Elevators	8
14.	Escalators	5

In a well-written paragraph, discuss one of the things you are most fearful of. Include reasons why you feel this way.

Sports Reports

Winning Ways

Newspaper sports pages are well read. Sports writers seem to learn the knack of making a faraway game seem close; for instance, they make you feel you're really seeing that touchdown scored in Edmonton. Sports writers write crisp, active prose. Their strong verbs and interesting adjectives make the game seem alive. Their crisp leads and their strong reliance on quotations also help make their writing exciting and true-to-life.

Dream comes true for Brian
Canadiens' unlikely hero sets a record in overtime
TONY FITZ-GERALD

CALGARY — The fifth wave of reporters had just vacated the area occupied by Brian Skrudland when a middle-aged man rushed into the Montreal dressing room and threw his arms around Canadiens' latest hero — his son.

The younger Skrudland had just realized his dream, a dream come true shared by millions of Canadian boys. He scored the winning goal, a mere nine seconds into overtime Sunday night, to give Canadiens a 3-2 win over Calgary Flames.

The best-of-seven Stanley Cup final now shifts to Montreal for game three tonight and game four Thursday night.

"It's a dream come true just to be in the position I'm in," Skrudland said. "I wouldn't have predicted this in 1000 years, especially with me scoring the winning goal. I wouldn't be in this position if it wasn't for a lot of hard work from guys I played with last year with the Sherbrooke Canadiens.

"It was always a dream of mine to be in this position. It was another dream to scoring the winning goal in overtime."

Record time

The goal not only evened the series at a game each, it put Skrudland in the record book.

"I was told it was a record," said the Canadiens' rookie centre. "One guy asked me if I remembered J.P. Parise because he had the 11 seconder."

The limelight has eluded Skrudland most of his career. He was the most valuable player in the American Hockey League's playoffs last year.

He had joined the Canadiens after being cut by the Olympic team in 1983. He was given little or no chance of making the Canadiens this year and when he did, spent a large amount of time on the bench.

"It's great to score with my father up there in the stands," he said. "I'll bet that section went crazy. I hope they weren't out getting hot dogs or Cokes because that was a big goal for me. I scored that for a lot of people."

Jays find the Key to winning ways
Solid win over Mariners a memory of better days
JEFF DICKINS

SEATTLE — Jimmy Key flexed his left arm — the limb that had been malfunctioning all year — and gave a small chuckle.

"Yeah, about time, eh. It feels a lot better than it has been."

The southpaw wasn't referring to his physical condition after Toronto's 4-3 victory over Seattle Mariners yesterday.

He was talking about mental health — both his and that of the up-and-more-often-down 13-18 Jays — after finally finding a consistent performance.

Key entered the game with six straight poor starts and not a solitary win. Coming into yesterday's contest he'd faced 103 hitters and 29 had eventually scored.

But only three of 30 Mariners he faced crossed the plate as Key's ERA dropped from 13.05 to a slightly more palatable 10.41.

Still, it wasn't easy.

After being staked to a 2-0 lead in the third, Key promptly ran into difficulties. A double, single, sacrifice fly, walk, double and single gave the Mariners a 3-2 edge.

Only a base-running mistake by the second man in the chain — Dave Henderson — prevented a bigger deficit.

But it was during that potential disaster that Key came up with a new scheme to avoid the familiar pitfall.

"It went through my head (deja vu), I can't deny that. I just had to try and forget about it."

That wasn't an easy task with slugger Gorman Thomas arriving at the plate licking his chops. There was the possibility of walking the heavy hitter and searching for a more likely victim.

Reverse

"I told Ernie (Whitt), 'Let's get him out. I don't need any more base-runners'."

The 25-year-old former all-star accomplished that by putting his past philosophy in reverse and adopting a new tactic.

"I went all the other way aggressive today after that — figured make them hit it and beat me."

Apparently Key, always a control pitcher, had become even more cautious than in 1985 when he went 14-6. And while he nibbled, opposition hitters were waiting patiently before chomping at his deliveries.

"It hadn't been working the other way, so why not try something different."

The change meant fastballs inside, what's commonly called challenging the hitter.

"I don't think I'll pitch that same way all year. But I had to get me out of that run of bad luck," he explained.

"The next time out I'll try and do what I did today — and see if it works."

BUILDING A WRITING CONTEXT

1. Which headline do you find more effective? Why?
2. Why do you think many newspaper headlines are followed by "sub-headlines?"
3. How do the sports writers make the athletes "come alive" for the readers?
4. List three strong verbs and three interesting adjectives found within these two articles.

THE WRITING WORKSHOP

Preparing to Write

In a group of three, read and discuss sports stories from your local newspaper. Look especially at the leads (introductions) the writers use, and how the rest of an article is somehow linked to this lead.

Look for effective verbs and adjectives used in various stories. Have one group member record these.

Discuss possible subjects for a sports article.

Think about school, local or national athletes, teams, or games. Possible subjects are: school soccer, NHL hockey, ladies' tennis, and CFL football. Decide on a general subject.

Developing the Writing

Now get more specific.

Decide what game or activity involving your subject you want to write about. Decide on a main idea for your story — a thesis to be developed. Use a chart like the one below:

General Subject:	Hockey
Topic:	Stanley Cup 1986, final game between Montreal Canadiens and Calgary Flames.
Main Idea (Thesis):	Montreal veterans lead band of rookies to Stanley Cup win.

Next plan your opening and closing paragraphs. A striking lead, or introduction, will spark the readers' interest. An effective conclusion will sum up the thesis or main idea in a clever and/or imaginative way.

To write a striking lead; you could do one or more of the following.

- Make a controversial statement.
- Relate a humorous story.
- Present an interesting quote.
- Ask a provocative question.

To end your report well, you could do one or more of the following.

- Make a comparison that emphasizes the thesis.
- Use a quote.

- Restate the thesis or main idea in a new way.
- Make a statement that ties directly back to the lead.

Write your first draft, developing your main idea with three or four paragraphs between the lead and the conclusion. Then write an effective headline.

Revising and Editing

A. With a partner revise your sports report. Discuss each of the following questions.
1. Is the main idea of interest?
2. Does the lead "grab" the reader's attention?
3. Is the main idea or thesis developed sufficiently?
4. Should some ideas and/or sentences be left out?
5. Are all paragraphs somehow connected to the thesis?
6. Are the words lively, especially the verbs and adjectives?
7. If quotes are used, are they appropriate?
8. Does the headline capture the central idea of the article?

B. Proofread your article using the checklist on page 145.

Sharing and Publishing

Work together to publish a class sports newspaper to be distributed to students and parents. You will need photographers, sports writers, editors, graphic artists, and ad people. Select a managing editor to coordinate the different tasks.

Growing from Writing

Read three different articles about the same sporting event. They should be from different newspapers or magazines. Note differences in:
- Main ideas.
- Relative importance of the article in relation to any other items on the same page.
- Whether accompanied by a photo or not.
- Effects of the headlines.
- Choice of words.

Present a brief oral report to your class, comparing the three articles.

Character Profiles

His Spirit Soared

One of the most visible and famous of Canada's Native people was Chief Dan George. Dan George was born in 1899 on the Burrard Reserve in North Vancouver, British Columbia. As a child, he learned the traditional ways of his people. Late in life he was elected a chief of the Squamish.

Always a spokesperson for his people, Dan George published two collections of meditations on Native people and the modern world. They are entitled *My Heart Soars* and *My Spirit Soars*. Following is a character profile of this famous actor, public speaker, author, and leader. It was written just a few years before his death in 1981.

Dan George

It is Academy Awards Night, 1971. Crowds of people are clamouring to see their favourite stars as they arrive and file into the Los Angeles Music Centre. Flash bulbs pop and spotlights play over the throngs picking out famous faces and award nominees. The tension builds as limousine after limousine glides up to the Music Center and lets out its own famous passengers. As each door is opened by a chauffeur, the crowd of onlookers press even closer to catch a glimpse of people they see normally only on the screen.

When the door of one particular limousine swings open, a small bronze-skinned, craggy-faced man with shoulder length silver hair steps spryly out to the sound of mild applause. The man squints in the glare of television lights and looks slightly uncomfortable. The Hollywood glamour and glitter is a long way from the world of Burrard Inlet, British Columbia, where Chief Dan George has lived all his life. After nodding slightly to acknowledge the crowd, the 71-year-old Co-Salish Indian moves in to take his seat at Hollywood's annual awards night.

As Dan George sits among the famous celebrities, the television cameras often zero in on his handsome, almost regal, face. Finally the moment comes. An actor on stage reads the list of nominees for Best Supporting Actor in 1970. Dan George's role as Ol' Lodgeskins in the film *Little Big Man* is described. Dan draws a breath of anticipation as the envelope is opened. The actor on stage utters the now famous words "And the winner is . . . ." There is a pause. Then the name follows. John Mills is named for his role in *Ryan's Daughter*. Dan George sits back in his seat almost relieved. At least the whole thing is over and he can return to the environment where he is most comfortable.

Dan lives in a small white cottage which overlooks the water on Burrard Reserve No. 3. He was born on the reserve in 1899 and has been there all his life. As a child, he lived as his people had always lived, helping his parents collect seafood and berries, preserving the food, and storing it away for winter use. He learned crafts and the traditional ways of the Co-Salish tribe. Until he was 16, he attended St. Paul's Boarding School in North Vancouver.

At 19, Dan George married Amy Jack, a beautiful girl from a neighbouring reserve and settled down to work. In 1920 he went to work on the British Columbia docks for 40 cents an hour. The work was hard and the days long. Toiling in groups of four, the men on the docks would pack 12 m lengths of timber and hoist them into the huge ships that came into port from all over the world. One day a swinging timber suddenly broke loose from a bundle, crashed into Dan and tossed him. It smashed all the muscles in his hip and left one leg shorter than the other. After 27 years, Dan George's working days on the docks had abruptly died.

But Dan's career was not yet over. After his accident he was elected chief of his tribe and, for the next 12 years, he dedicated much of his time to the work of leading his people. He was voted out of office in 1963. Since then he has been named

Honorary Chief of both the Shuswap and Squamish tribes.

The other career that began when Dan lost his job on the docks was as an entertainer. Soon he was known locally in Burrard Inlet. His real break came in 1960, when he was approached to fill the role of Antoine on the CBC television series *Cariboo Country*. Over the next five years, he became deeply involved with television and professional theatre work. He also performed on radio and gained a reputation as a public speaker.

With his appearance in Walt Disney's film *How to Break a Quarter Horse* he made his entrance into motion pictures in the United States. Since then he has worked on American television and stage. His experience with *Little Big Man* and the Academy Awards left him bruised, however. The $16 000 that he received for the movie part turned out to be a fraction of the figure that had been offered other actors for the same role. And when he didn't win an Oscar he realized how fickle the world of Hollywood could be. "I'm glad in a way that he didn't get it," remembers his friend, broadcaster Hilda Mortimer. She was one of the people who accompanied Dan to the Awards ceremony and saw how he was treated. "We sat in a room together the next day and waited for all those promised people who never came. The magazines. The agents. The studio people."

Perhaps, though, it is another aspect of his career that has become most significant. He is well known as a spokesman for the Indian people. His wise countenance and unique husky whisper combine to command almost immediate attention and respect. His habit of punctuating his soft-spoken words with pauses of silence has a spellbinding effect. "Years ago, I dedicated myself to try to do something that would give a name to the Indian people," Dan has said. It may be that his public speaking is doing as much for this goal as his acting career.

A particularly fine example of Dan George's effectiveness as a speaker was illustrated on July 1, 1967, when he spoke in Vancouver's Empire Stadium to a crowd of 32 000 people. The occasion, of course, was Canada's centennial celebration and the milling throng that had gathered was in a buoyant holiday mood. It took the Chief only minutes to achieve complete silence and seriousness among the celebrating Canadians as he delivered an eloquent but bitter "Lament for Confederation" in which he poignantly stated that Canada's first 100 years had not been good to the Indian people.

And so it is not surprising that Dan George still lives on the reserve at Burrard Inlet in his little white cottage far from the fast-moving world of Hollywood. Leaving the reserve, he feels, is for another generation. For him it is home and he is happy to be with his people.

BUILDING A WRITING CONTEXT

1. **Obtain a map of the Vancouver area. Locate Burrard Inlet and the various Indian reserves in that area.**
2. **In your opinion, what personality traits led Chief Dan George to be such a respected man?**
3. **Think about prejudice in TV programs and in movies. What programs have you seen that were unfair in their presentation of Native North Americans? Why did you think they were unfair? Discuss a program that gave, in your opinion, an honest treatment of Native life, either of the past or the present.**

THE WRITING WORKSHOP

Preparing to Write

Read brief biographies of five famous and/or infamous people. You may find these in encyclopedias and other reference works. As you read, list several clues as to each person's identity. Examples: I am a German composer. I was born in 1770.

Choose one set of clues and read them to the class or to a group, keeping your famous person's name a secret. Start with the hardest clue, and see how long it takes your classmates to guess the person's name.

If there is time, you may go on to read a second set of clues. Or you and a classmate could exchange sets of clues, read them, and try to guess each other's famous people.

In preparing your clues, you may wish to choose some names from the following list.

1. Lucy Maud Montgomery
2. Adolf Hitler
3. Rasputin
4. Jack the Ripper
5. John A. Macdonald
6. King Henry VIII

7. Anne Murray
8. Count Dracula
9. Indira Gandhi
10. Joan of Arc
11. Jacques Cartier
12. Edward Teach (Blackbeard)
13. Poundmaker
14. John F. Kennedy
15. Robin Hood
16. Anne Frank
17. Baroness Maria Von Trapp
18. Pierre Trudeau
19. A.Y. Jackson
20. Queen Elizabeth II
21. Percy Bysshe Shelley
22. Florence Nightingale
23. Bertrand Russell
24. Babe Ruth
25. Pablo Picasso
26. Albert Schweitzer
27. Michelangelo
28. Marie Antoinette
29. Martin Luther
30. Thomas Edison
31. Margaret Laurence
32. Ludwig van Beethoven
33. Napoleon Bonaparte
34. Leonardo da Vinci
35. Attila the Hun
36. Marie Curie
37. Joseph Stalin
38. Christopher Columbus
39. Laura Secord
40. Robert Burns
41. Louis Riel
42. Sitting Bull
43. Pauline Johnson
44. Billy Bishop
45. Sarah Bernhardt
46. Louis Braille
47. Helen Keller
48. Edgar Allan Poe
49. Julius Caesar
50. Emily Murphy
51. William Shakespeare
52. Stephen Leacock
53. Norman Bethune
54. Golda Meir
55. George Bernard Shaw
56. Kateri Tekakwitha
57. Nero
58. Chief Crowfoot
59. Father Albert Lacombe
60. Emily Carr

Developing the Writing

A. Select one of the famous or infamous people from the above list (or think of one of your own). Choose an important moment in that person's life, and write a dramatic scene (or short story) about it.

B. Write a profile of an imaginary person who has all or most of the qualities you most admire. Perhaps this could be the person you would (now or someday) like to be.

C. Often we are all guilty of prejudging, or "stereotyping" an individual. In sizing people up we all fall back now and then on certain outward signs of inner character. Write a character sketch or story that *disproves* one of the following common beliefs, or a common belief of your own choice. You could write about either a real or an imaginary person.

1. Long, slender hands mean an artistic temperament.
2. Redheaded people are more temperamental than others.
3. A person who does not look you in the eye is likely to be dishonest.
4. A receding chin shows lack of willpower.
5. Blondes are likely to be less trustworthy than brunettes.
6. Stout people are typically good-natured.
7. Ears pointed at the top warn of sneakiness, selfishness, or even dishonesty.
8. Wrinkles at the outer corners of the eyes show that a person has a sense of humour.
9. Curly hair is a sign of exuberance and vitality.
10. A high, bulging forehead is a sign of superior brainpower.
11. Cold hands are a sign of an affectionate disposition.

D. Write a character profile of one of the following.

1. A person I have almost forgotten.
2. A person I can't bear.
3. My favourite teacher (relative, musician, athlete).
4. The most wonderful person I know.
5. My ancestor.
6. My best friend.
7. A person who has influenced my life.
8. A prominent citizen in my home town.
9. The most disreputable person I ever met.
10. A person who never had a chance.
11. An interesting public personality.
12. A character from fiction — someone I'd like to meet.

Revising and Editing

Choose one piece of writing that you did in this chapter. Write a final draft of it, to be given to your teacher for evaluation. As you edit your work before writing the final draft, you may wish to consider adding relevant information about some or all of the following topics.

- Subject's physical self: appearance, health, dress, way of moving, and so on.
- Subject's psychological self: possibly including the person's attitudes towards others, work, morals, law, religion, life in general.

- Subject's background: perhaps including nationality, race, parentage, place and circumstances of birth, siblings, relatives, social and economic standing, friends and enemies.
- Important dates in the person's life.
- Your opinion on what kind of an individual the person is or was.

Sharing and Publishing

Give the final draft of your chosen piece of writing to your teacher.

Growing from Writing

A. Find and browse through one or both of Chief Dan George's books: *My Heart Soars* and *My Spirit Soars.*

B. What is heroism in our day? Who are today's heroes? Probably they include astronauts, athletes, politicians, military figures, missionaries, performers, humble and unknown people of heroic stature. Write a brief poem about a modern-day hero, showing this person in action. Be specific and detailed.

If you find this assignment difficult, start by listing your details in brief sentences or phrases, one to a line. You may be surprised to see how much like a poem your writing looks and reads. Polish it until you are satisfied with it.

Speeches

Ruthie's Promise

In the life of a Jewish girl, the day of her bat mitzvah is a most important occasion. Bat mitzvah — a religious ceremony marking a girl's entry into the responsibilities of adulthood — takes place when she is about 13. On the day of her bat mitzvah, the Jewish girl becomes an adult in the eyes of her family, friends, Rabbi, and God. As part of the ceremony the girl must present a speech to her congregation. Below is such a speech, given by a girl named Ruthie.

from **Daughters-in-Law** HENRY CECIL

After more reading and prayers, Ruthie stepped to the pulpit to begin her speech. This, she had confessed, was the hardest part of all, to gather her feelings about this momentous occasion and express them in her own words in front of everyone.

"Beloved Rabbi, Mama, Aunt Sarah, and dear friends," she began. She blinked several times and Denise crossed her fingers in her lap, all of them, including her thumbs. After a deep breath, Ruthie continued:

"This day marks the beginning of my adulthood according to Jewish law. From now on, I am responsible for my actions, my decisions, my physical and spiritual well-being. I know this will not be easy, because a couple of months ago, I was faced with the decision of whether or not even to have a bat mitzvah, and it was very hard. But I have learned that hard things, difficult and painful things, help us to grow. Through them, we increase our wisdom and understanding. By avoiding them, we get nowhere.

"This is supposed to be a joyous occasion, a celebration of life. After all my family had suffered, I wondered if there was a point in rejoicing. Was it even *right*? Sometimes I felt sure it was not right. There could be no more joy after such incredible pain. Other times, I thought, yes, we must go on, louder and stronger than before, to show that we're not defeated. But most of the time, I didn't know which way to go. In fact, most of this spring was spent going around in circles."

Ruthie smiled and the congregation chuckled softly in response. Denise felt the muscles of her stomach relax at last. She glanced sideways at her mother, so pretty in her new beige dress, and received a cheering wink.

"I circled around," Ruthie went on, "going over and over my past and my possible future and all that they meant and could mean. And, at last, with the help of Rabbi Davis, my mother, my Aunt Sarah, and my friends the Rileys, difficult things finally became simple and puzzling things became clear. First of all, I realized, I am alive. This is a fact. And I'm alive because of my parents, my aunt and uncle, and God. And, for the same reasons, I am Jewish. And, for still the same reasons, I am very lucky. My history goes back beyond the Holocaust to many other persecutions, and to many other triumphs over them. Yes, I have suffered the pain of my ancestors. But I am also strong with their enduring strength. My parents were survivors. I'm a survivor, too. We all are, because any evil hurts more than its immediate victims; it hurts the human race.

"But we have survived. We are alive and there is a lot to celebrate. I, personally, celebrate today the love and determination of my parents and my aunt and uncle, who gave me life and brought me to this moment of adulthood. And I celebrate the friendship of Mr. and Mrs. Riley and Denise, who showed me something very new: how warm and full of fun life could be when you share it with loving friends. And I celebrate the patient teaching of Rabbi Davis, who helped me to see the value, the importance of my existence. Every good life, he told me not long ago, is a triumph over evil. Well, I am here, I am alive, and I am grateful. And my first adult promise is to try my very best to lead a good life."

BUILDING A WRITING CONTEXT

1. **How did Ruthie feel about making a speech? Why do you think she felt this way?**
2. **Ruthie said she was not sure whether or not to go ahead with her bat mitzvah. Why was this?**
3. **Ruthie said she had much to celebrate. What were some of the things she celebrated in her speech?**

THE WRITING WORKSHOP

Preparing to Write

Three types of speeches are described below.
1. **The Humorous Speech**
   The purpose of this type of speech is to make an audience laugh. Example: stand-up comedy monologue.
   - Humorous stories and anecdotes help to make a speech entertaining. Examples of topics that might be treated humorously would include: your family, news of the day, fads, pets, sports, characters we all know, advertisers.
   - Satire, exaggeration, understatement, and description are some of the "tools" used in humorous speeches.
2. **The Informative Speech**
   This type of speech tells an audience about facts, findings, and/or experiences. The emphasis is on sharing information. Information should be gathered from a variety of sources, and the topic should be of interest to the speech-maker. Example: travel talk.
3. **The Persuasive Speech**
   The persuasive speech presents certain beliefs and/or ideas in such a way as to try to convince the audience to agree with them. Examples: sermon; political speech.

Developing the Writing

Once you decide on a kind of speech to give, use the following steps to write it.
1. **Choosing A Topic**
   - Select a topic that interests you, and that you believe will interest the audience.

- The topic should be specific — not too wide, yet not too narrow. A topic such as *television* might be too broad, while the topic *my favourite television personality* would probably be specific enough.
- You may wish to choose one of the following topics.
  - Halifax (or some other city) as a vacation spot.
  - Why a good worker may not be a good boss.
  - Why I enjoy living in a small town (or in a city, or on a farm).
  - Comparison of drunk and sober drivers.
  - Evils and virtues of competition.
  - A dog's life.
  - The ideal school.
  - Contrasts between really living and merely existing.

2. **Gathering Information**

   What are the main points you want to talk about? Brainstorm a list of ideas relating to your topic. Don't stop. Write as quickly as you can, recording all ideas, no matter how silly they may seem. (You can sort them later.)

   For some speeches you may also need to do research. Add the researched facts and ideas to your list.

3. **Writing the Speech**

   Next organize your brainstormed and researched material into a first draft of your speech. It is at this stage that you will evaluate and sort the results of your brainstorming — making use of what is appropriate and leaving out what is not.

   As you write your speech, follow the plan below.

   - **Introduction**

     The introduction lets the audience know what your speech is about. Your introduction should be interesting so that it will catch the audience's attention. It should be short, and can be developed in one of the following ways.
     - Ask a challenging question.
     - Tell a story of human interest, paint a "word picture," or give an illustration.
     - Use a statement that excites attention, arouses curiosity, surprises the audience, or is particularly informative.
     - Tell a humorous story related to the subject.
     - State facts showing the importance of the subject to the welfare of the audience.
     - Begin with a quotation or idea from some other person.

- **Body**

  The body is the main part of the speech. It tells the audience what the speaker wants them to know about the topic. It contains the main points with examples and details. It should be filled with facts and concrete illustrations, and not simply with generalities. The following ideas can help you write the body of your speech.
  - Facts, figures, and/or illustrations should be used to support the main points.
  - If you are preparing a persuasive speech in which the audience is to be convinced of some idea, begin with information with which there is general agreement. In this way you may lull the audience into accepting other ideas as well.

- **Conclusion**

  The conclusion should be short, and should re-emphasize or summarize the points developed in the body of the speech. The ending, like the beginning, should be memorable so as to leave a lasting impression with the audience. The following suggestions may help you conclude your speech:
  - You could tell a humorous story or close with a suitable witty comment.
  - The major points of the body could be outlined concisely.
  - You could ask the audience to take some form of action or to adopt a certain viewpoint on some matter.
  - You could use a quotation from the Bible or other literature if it is fitting.

Revising and Editing

With a partner revise and refine your speech with care. First be sure your ideas are presented clearly. Then examine your style and wording for effectiveness. Use the questions and guidelines below.
- Is the opening effective?
- Is the closing memorable?
- Are the points in the body of the speech developed clearly and logically? Does each have effective supporting details?

- Do you avoid using jargon unless you explain unusual terms so that the audience understands them?
- Do you avoid using slang unless it is an essential part of the speech or anecdote?
- Do you intersperse short sentences with long ones?
- Do you, if appropriate, sometimes use a series of short crisp sentences for emphasis and effectiveness?
- Do you, if appropriate, occasionally use similes, metaphors, and alliteration?
- Do you use appropriate antonyms to contrast ideas?
- Do you repeat some words or phrases for emphasis?

Sharing and Publishing

The delivery of a speech is the culmination of all the thought, research, and preparation that has gone into it. The use of voice, pronunciation, gesture, and posture are important elements of delivering your speech. As you present your speech to the class or to a group, keep the following guidelines in mind.

- **Voice**
  - It should be loud enough to be heard, but you should not shout.
  - It should be pleasant, and used in a relaxed and natural manner.
  - Volume, pitch, and rate should be varied according to the material presented in the speech.

- **Posture and Gestures**

In public speaking, non-verbal language and body action should be natural. The body should be used *with* the voice, to increase the effectiveness of the speech.

Good posture is essential.

- Stand straight.
- Feet should be kept apart, with one foot slightly forward.
- Avoid frequent shifting from one foot to the other. However, you may change your position from time to time.
- Avoid leaning on objects and fidgeting with notes, objects, or clothing.
- Effective eye contact is important when speaking in public. Look directly at the audience. Attention should be shifted from one area of the audience to another, but not too rapidly.

- Avoid frequently looking at the floor, the ceiling, or one particular section of the audience.
- Smile at the listeners from time to time, to help retain interest and rapport.

The speaker should use movements or gestures to emphasize, to describe, to point out, and to express emotion. Gestures should be natural. They should follow the thoughts of the speaker. For example, a speaker may fling his or her arm wide to indicate vast space. He or she may step forward boldly to indicate the need for bold action on the part of the audience.

Growing from Writing

A. Research the bat mitzvah and bar mitzvah ceremonies of the Jewish faith, and the confirmation ceremonies used in many Christian churches. In a one-page paper, describe some of the similarities and differences.

B. What is a professional speech-writer? Find out about this profession. Write a job description for such a person.

Free Verse

Part Vulture, Part Wolf

An appealing feature of free verse is that the poet is at liberty to express feelings and ideas without being restricted by the "rules" of traditional metrical forms. In free verse the poet develops his or her own rules of form for each new poem written.

Traditional poetry usually has a set form. It is organized in set stanzas having regular rhythm patterns and often regular rhyme schemes. Free verse has none of these restrictions. The lines have no set length in terms of a fixed number of syllables. Free verse lacks the predictable rhythms established by a predetermined metrical pattern. Rhyming is optional and frequently occurs in the form of internal and half rhymes rather than end-line rhymes. A great deal of modern poetry is free verse.

Fog
Carl Sandburg

The fog comes
on little cat feet.

It sits looking
over harbour and city
on silent haunches
and then moves on.

How to Eat a Poem
Eve Merriam

Don't be polite.
Bite in.
Pick it up with your fingers and lick the juice that
    may run down your chin.
It is ready and ripe now, whenever you are.

You do not need a knife or fork or spoon
or plate or napkin or tablecloth.

For there is no core
or stem
or rind
or pit
or seed
or skin
to throw away.

Kittens
Katherine Anastasio, St. Margaret Mary School

Multi-coloured coats,
Soft as a whisper,
Fluffy as a cloud,
Inquisitive
As toddlers on the run,
Sincere faces,
Eyes,
Shining like the sun,
Awkward little kittens.
Soon,
Elegant cats.

The Shark
E.J. Pratt

He seemed to know the harbour,
So leisurely he swam;
His fin,
Like a piece of sheet-iron,
Three-cornered,
And with knife-edge,
Stirred not a bubble
As it moved
With its base-line on the water.

His body was tubular
And tapered
And smoke-blue,
And as he passed the wharf
He turned,
And snapped at a flat-fish
That was dead and floating.
And I saw the flash of a white throat,
And a double row of white teeth,
And eyes of metallic gray,
Hard and narrow and slit.

Then out of the harbour,
With that three-cornered fin
Shearing without a bubble the water
Lithely,
Leisurely,
He swam —
That strange fish,
Tubular, tapered, smoke-blue,
Part vulture, part wolf,
Part neither for his blood was cold.

BUILDING A WRITING CONTEXT

1. The poem "Fog" is a metaphor comparing fog to a cat.
   List several ways in which fog and a cat might be alike.
   Do you like the image created by the metaphor? Why or
   why not?

2. What is the metaphor in "How To Eat A Poem?" In a paragraph, explain the following statement: Writing a free verse poem is in some ways like eating a grapefruit without paying attention to table manners.
3. Why are the similes used in "Kittens" appropriate? How is the last line of this poem a contrast to the rest of the poem?
4. What three adjectives in stanza three of "The Shark" seem to compare the fish's body to the barrel of a gun? In what ways is the shark like a vulture?

THE WRITING WORKSHOP

Preparing to Write

You too can write a free verse poem. As a poet, you can touch someone in a powerful way with your ideas and feelings. Your poem can form part of a class booklet to be read by other students.

Reread several of the free verse poems presented in this chapter before you try to write one of your own. Pay special attention to the form of each poem. Note the wide variety of line lengths, and the lack of end rhyme.

Developing the Writing

One of the best ways to get started on your poem is to take a colourful and descriptive selection from a story and turn it into free verse. Poetic writing is sometimes present in what is usually called *prose*. Often a piece of prose just needs to be rearranged into a different form to become a free verse poem. Here are some suggestions to consider:

1. The descriptive prose piece you select can be on any topic. It could be from a novel, a short story, a science or history text, or a magazine or newspaper article. Possible topics include: A Haunted House, A Science Experiment, A Battle in The War of 1812, A Character Description.
2. Be sure the prose selection is complete in itself and not too long.
3. Underline or list key words and phrases in the selection.

4. Organize into lines of poetry these words and phrases, as well as any others you find appropriate. Lines can be one word to several words long. The line length should be determined by the power of the image being presented. One-word lines, for example, can be used to give emphasis to single words.
5. Leave out all unnecessary words.
6. Use similes and metaphors when appropriate.
7. Using only present tense verbs in your poems helps create a unity of time as well as a sense of immediacy in your work. Try using this technique.
8. Add other descriptive words and phrases that strengthen your image. You might repeat certain words and phrases to add emphasis to important ideas.

Now, considering the above suggestions, write your free verse poem based on a prose selection.

Revising and Editing

A. Reread your poem and edit it using the questions below:
• Does my poem deal with my topic in a way that is interesting, unusual, and powerful? If not, how can I make my poem stronger?
• Can I leave out any words to achieve a "tighter" effect?
• Should I alter my line arrangements to place more emphasis on certain words?
• Have I used a consistent verb tense throughout, unless there was a specific reason to change tense?

B. Use of Punctuation and Line Length for Effect

In free verse poetry the placement of a comma, the subtle use of a dash, or the organization of lines can have an important effect on the overall meaning and impact. Edit with a partner, discussing especially how best to use punctuation and line length to achieve your desired effect.

Sharing and Publishing

Write the final draft of your poem, and give it to your teacher for inclusion in a class anthology. You might consider working with several other students to help compile the anthology.

Growing from Writing

Just as you have used a descriptive prose selection to write a free verse poem, use an especially effective free verse poem to write a prose selection. Once you have selected the poem, select the prose form suitable to your purpose. Use, for example, a paragraph, letter, note, essay, report, or experimental form. When completed, have the poem and your prose selection read by a friend. Discuss with your friend similarities and differences between the two pieces of writing.

Narrative Poems

Running the Long Soo

Long ago people began telling stories of great deeds and heroes through ballads. The earliest ballads were usually sung to audiences rather than written down. Later, poets used the ballad form to create written poems. They often shared their written ballads by reading or speaking them aloud.

Today we can listen to recordings of a wide variety of modern ballads. Folk, country, and rock ballads are popular. As in the past, ballads tell interesting stories.

ELEANOR RIGBY
John Lennon and Paul McCartney

Eleanor Rigby —
Picks up the rice in the church where a wedding has been;
Lives in a dream.
Waits at the window,
Wearing a face that she keeps in a jar by the door —
Who is it for?

All the lonely people!
Where do they all come from?
All the lonely people!
Where do they all belong?

Father Mackenzie —
Writing the words of a sermon that no one will hear;
No one comes near.
Look at him working
Darning his socks in the night when there's nobody
    there—
What does he care?

All the lonely people!
Where do they all come from?
All the lonely people!
Where do they all belong?

Eleanor Rigby —
Died in the church and was buried along with her name —
Nobody came!
Father Mackenzie —
Wiping the dirt from his hands as he walks from the grave —
No one was saved!

All the lonely people!
Where do they all come from?
All the lonely people!
Where do they all belong?

Ye Maidens of Ontario

Ye maidens of Ontario, give ear to what I write,
In driving down these rapid streams where raftsmen take
    delight,
In driving down these rapid streams as jolly raftsmen do,
While your lowland loafing farmer boys can stay at home with
    you.

These lowland loafing farmer boys, they tell the girls great tales
Of all the dangers they go through in crossing o'er their fields.
The cutting of the grass so green is all that they can do,
While we poor jolly raftsmen are running the Long Soo.

And when the sun is going down, their plows they'll cast aside.
They'll jump upon their horses' backs and homeward they will
    ride,
And when the clock strikes eight or nine, then into bed they'll
    crawl,
While down on Lake St. Peter we stand many a bitter squall.

The wind blew from the south and east; it blew our cribs along.
It blew so very hard it shook our timbers up and down,
And put us in confusion for fear we should all drown.
Our pilot cried, "Cheer up, brave boys! Your red pine oars
    bring on."

When we get down to Quebec town, the girls all dance for joy.
Says one unto another one, "Here comes a shanty boy!"
One treats us to a bottle, and another to a dram,
While toasts go 'round the table for the jolly shanty man.

Before I'd been in Quebec long — in weeks 'twas scarcely three,
The landlord's lovely daughter did fall in love with me.
She told me that she loved me, and she took me by the hand,
And shyly told her mother that she loved a shanty man.

"O daughter, dearest daughter, you grieve my heart full sore,
To fall in love with a shanty man you never saw before."
"Well, mother, I don't care for that, so do the best you can,
For I'm bound to go to Ottawa with my roving shanty man."

BUILDING A WRITING CONTEXT

1. "Eleanor Rigby" is about isolation, loneliness, and the
   lack of communication in our world. What is so sad
   about Eleanor Rigby picking up the rice after the
   wedding? How is she similar to Father Mackenzie?
2. Old ballads usually have a regular number of lines in
   each stanza with a regular rhyme pattern. Ballads also
   have regular rhythm patterns. This means that the
   accents of the syllables in the words fall at regular
   intervals, like the beat in music. Referring to "Ye
   Maidens of Ontario," answer the following questions:
   • How many lines are in each stanza of this poem?
   • How do the lines rhyme in most stanzas?

- Count the stressed syllables or beats in various lines. How many are there?

THE WRITING WORKSHOP

Preparing to Write

Read again the ballads in this chapter, focusing on the story in each. Narratives (stories) have plot, character, setting, conflict, and theme. Since ballads are narrative poems, they contain the elements of stories.

With a partner discuss story elements contained in the ballads in this chapter.

Developing the Writing

1. Brainstorm with a partner possible topics for a ballad of your own. You might consider one of the following ideas:
   - Write "Ye Maidens of Ontario" from a different point of view, perhaps from the point of view of a trustworthy, settled farmboy.
   - Write a ballad about a person who lives a lonely life isolated from society.
2. Once you decide on a topic, brainstorm words and ideas for your ballad under the headings below.

Main Events or Plot	Character	Setting	Conflict

Theme _____

3. Reread your lists. Add, leave out, and rearrange words and ideas as necessary. Use any symbols that work to help you organize your ideas; for example, arrows, circles, underlining, numbers.
4. Next borrow rhyme and rhythm patterns from one of the ballads in this chapter, or experiment with patterns of your own until you find those that are "right" for your ballad.
5. Now write your first draft. Focus on telling your story. Don't spend too much time on your rhyme and rhythm patterns at this point. You can work more on these later.

82

Revising and Editing

A. Revise your poem using these questions:
- Is my story complete? Does it have all the elements of a good story?
- Should I add or leave out anything to improve my story?
- For the sake of my rhyme and rhythm patterns, have I written lines that sound "forced," or that don't quite make sense? How can I improve these?

B. **Rhyme and Rhythm**

Rhyme is an important device in poetry. It adds to the musical sound of a poem and hence is important in writing ballads. Generally speaking, rhyme occurs when two words have the same final vowel sound. For example, *day* rhymes with *play*. There are several types of rhyme. The most common form is end rhyme, which is the rhyme that occurs at the ends of lines.

Rhythm is something like beat in music. A line of poetry often has a set number of strong and weak syllables that produce a "beat."

For example:
   All the lonely people!
   Where do they all come from?
   All the lonely people!
   Where do they all belong?

In this stanza, each line has three "beats." Examine other stanzas in "Eleanor Rigby" to see if the same rhythm pattern is used in each. How does this rhythm pattern contribute to the wistful thoughtfulness of the poem?

With a partner edit your ballad, helping one another to use rhyme and rhythm to add to the story told.

Sharing and Publishing

Write your final draft in your best handwriting. In a group of four, read your poem aloud. After all four poems have been read, discuss what you enjoyed about each. Keep your ballad in your writing folder. You might decide to submit it for publication in a class anthology.

Growing from Writing

A. Write a different ending to the ballad "Ye Maidens of Ontario." Tell what happened to the shanty man and the daughter when they got to Ottawa. Write at least one more stanza to give this poem a different ending. Use the same rhyme and rhythm pattern as in the other stanzas.

B. Bring to class the Beatles' album *Revolver* on Capitol Records. Listen to the ballad "Eleanor Rigby" and in a group discuss how the theme of loneliness is heightened by the choice of instruments and by the rhythm.

Formula Poems

A Fair-Headed Maiden of Klondike

Formula poems are written to a specific pattern or formula. They are usually concise statements that comment on the ordinary in extraordinary ways.

A. Three-Word Model

Lions	Hawks	Wind
Laugh	Hunt	Whistles
Loudly	Hungrily	Wildly

This concise poetry pattern is known as the *three-word model or the noun-verb-adverb model*. A noun, verb, and adverb (in that order) are listed vertically. The three words together should make an interesting or unusual statement about the topic (the first word). Notice that all three words begin with the same letter. This use of alliteration gives the poem a unifying link.

Write a three-word model poem on a topic of your choice, or use one of these nouns to get started: motorcycles, wolves, rain, spiders.

Be sure that the adverb you select is appropriate, given the meaning and feeling you want to express.

B. Concrete Poems

Rubik's Cube
Paul Salvo, St. Mary's High School

```
RUBIK
    N
    V
    E   L
    N   I
    THAT
    E   T
    D   L
      BEFUDDLING
        R
      CUBE
        S
        T
        R
        A
        THAT
        I   E
        N   ME        I
        G   P         N
            T OWARDS
            S         A
                      N
                      I
                      T
                      Y
```

```
        GOLDEN
    WARM       LARGE
        SUN
    BRIGHT     ROUND
```

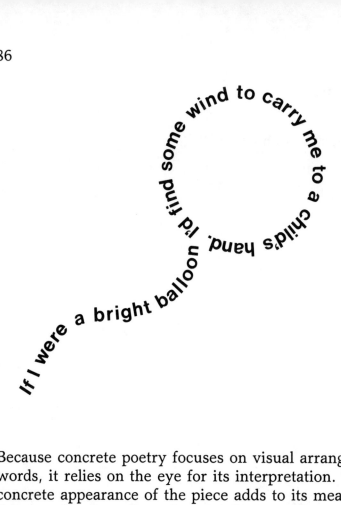

If I were a bright balloon, I'd find some wind to carry me to a child's hand.

Because concrete poetry focuses on visual arrangements of words, it relies on the eye for its interpretation. The shape or concrete appearance of the piece adds to its meaning. How is this true for the poems above? Select one style of concrete poetry. Create a concrete poem using a topic of your choice.

C. Diamante

Circle

birth
miraculous, joyous
growing, living, loving
life, youth, growth, time
remembering, giving, aging
gracious, dignified
death

A diamond-shaped poem such as this is called *diamante*. The pattern was created by Iris M. Tiedt. Think about its characteristics:

- The diamante is a seven-line poem.
- Line 1 — one word, a noun.

- Line 2 — two adjectives describing the word in line 1.
- Line 3 — three participles (words ending in -ing or -ed) that tell about the noun.
- Line 4 — four nouns related to the subject.
- Line 5 — three or more participles (-ing or -ed) that tell about the second two nouns in line 4.
- Line 6 — two adjectives describing the second two nouns in line 5.
- Line 7 — one word, a noun, opposite in meaning to the noun in line 1.

The result is a seven-line contrast poem that has changed in meaning from beginning to end.

D. Limerick

A boy with a stick and a puck
Was skating when he suddenly got stuck.
He said, "Some old bum,
Threw out his old gum,"
So all night he was stuck in that guck.

> Christopher Tihor
> Holy Name of Jesus School

Said a fair-headed maiden of Klondike
"Of you I'm exceedingly fond, Ike.
To prove I adore you
I'll dye, darling, for you
And be a brunette, not a blonde, Ike."

> Traditional

The limerick was first a kind of song. Limericks became popular when Edward Lear published his *Book of Nonsense* in 1846. To write a limerick you must follow a definite rhyme scheme and rhythm pattern.

Limericks usually follow the pattern outlined below.
- A limerick is a five-line poem.
- Lines 3 and 4 rhyme.
- Lines 1, 2, and 5 rhyme.
- Lines 1, 2, and 5 have three strong beats.

88

- Lines 3 and 4 have two strong beats.
- A limerick is a nonsense poem.

Also:
- Line 1 — tells something about the subject and perhaps where he or she is from.
- Line 2 — describes the person or some action of his or hers.
- Line 3 and 4 — continues the idea about the subject mentioned in the second line.
- Line 5 — concludes the poem with a funny or unexpected ending.

With a partner write a limerick to share with the class. Use one of these first lines if you wish.

There once was a girl from North Bay

A teacher from Vancouver Island

A Calgary lad drove his car

THE WRITING WORKSHOP

Preparing to Write

Read again the formula poems on pages 84-87, and those you composed. Study the patterns. You will be writing several pattern poems to display on a wall or bulletin board in your school. You will want these poems to interest and perhaps amuse your readers.

Developing the Writing

1. Select a topic for your series of formula poems. Ordinary topics such as tropical fish, school, record albums, and milk can be made extraordinary by a clever poet. Be that creative word magician. Write one three-word model, one concrete, one diamante, and one limerick about your topic. If you wish, add to this collection one or two other types of formula poems you are familiar with (for example, acrostic, four-line descriptive model, adverb model, haiku, cinquain).
2. Once you select a topic, brainstorm words and ideas on a piece of paper. Next, try to arrange these words and ideas around four or more subheadings which can become the

topics of each poem. Add other ideas. Each cluster of ideas could then be worked into a different formula poem.

3. Your brainstorming on a topic such as *milk* might result in the following writing plan.

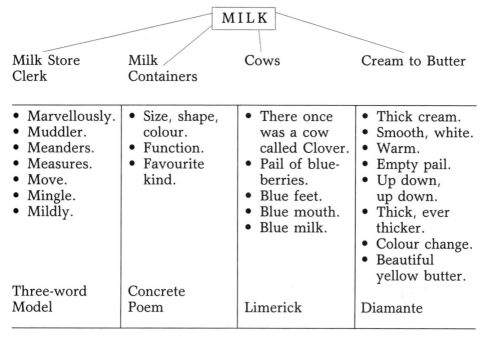

MILK			
Milk Store Clerk	**Milk Containers**	**Cows**	**Cream to Butter**
• Marvellously. • Muddler. • Meanders. • Measures. • Move. • Mingle. • Mildly.	• Size, shape, colour. • Function. • Favourite kind.	• There once was a cow called Clover. • Pail of blueberries. • Blue feet. • Blue mouth. • Blue milk.	• Thick cream. • Smooth, white. • Warm. • Empty pail. • Up down, up down. • Thick, ever thicker. • Colour change. • Beautiful yellow butter.
Three-word Model	Concrete Poem	Limerick	Diamante

4. Based on your plan, write your poems.

Revising and Editing

A. Read your four poems again and revise each as necessary, using the questions below.

- Does my poem explore my topic in a way that is interesting, unusual, or powerful? If not, how can I add impact to my writing?
- Are all my words and phrases directly related to my topic?
- Are my words and phrases the most accurate and most interesting I could use to communicate my meaning?
- Should I add ideas, leave out ideas, or rearrange ideas to create a more powerful effect?

B. **Effective Diction**

Good poetry uses the fewest possible words to communicate subtle meanings and feelings. Only the most exact and powerful words for a given situation should be used. The dictionary, the thesaurus, and our classmates can help us make effective word choices.

Good diction is effective word choice.

Exchange your poems with another student, and edit one another's work. Look especially for *effective diction* by focusing on the words — what they say and how forcefully they say it. Suggest that all unnecessary words be deleted. You could discuss possible words and phrases to replace any that are inaccurate or weak.

Sharing and Publishing

Publish your final drafts on one or more sheets of paper and add any suitable artwork. You can contribute to a class display on a bulletin board or wall. Take some time to enjoy the poems of your classmates. They too will enjoy reading your work. Later these published pieces can be placed in your writing folder.

Growing from Writing

A. In a group of four refer to various poetry anthologies and other sources of published poetry to develop a collection of favourite limericks. Organize these in a booklet or on a display board and encourage your classmates to enjoy this poetry.

B. Memorize a limerick you particularly enjoy, and recite it to the class.

Lyric Poetry

Go, Cat, Go!

The word *lyric* is often used to refer to the words of a song. Long ago this meant a song sung with a lyre. A lyre is an old Greek musical instrument that looks something like a small harp. Today the word *lyric* refers not only to words of a song, but also to a type of poetry.

Lyric poems emphasize feelings. They might also tell a story, but the story is not the most important aspect of the lyric poem. In this way lyric poems differ from narrative poems.

The poems that follow all describe ordinary things in unordinary ways. In each case the author expresses strong feelings about a topic. The song "Blue Suede Shoes" is an enjoyable example of a modern lyric meant to be sung.

Steam Shovel
Charles Malam

The dinosaurs are not all dead.
I saw one raise its iron head
To watch me walking down the road
Beyond our house today.
Its jaws were dripping with a load
Of earth and grass that it had cropped.
It must have heard me where I stopped,
Snorted white steam my way,
And stretched its long neck out to see,
And chewed, and grinned quite amiably.

The Eagle
Alfred, Lord Tennyson

He clasps the crag with crooked hands;
Close to the sun in lonely lands.
Ring'd with the azure world, he stands.

The wrinkled sea beneath him crawls;
He watches from his mountain walls,
And like a thunderbolt he falls.

Dreams
Langston Hughes

Hold fast to dreams
For if dreams die
Life is a broken-winged bird
That cannot fly.

Hold fast to dreams
For when dreams go
Life is a barren field
Frozen with snow.

A Thunderstorm
Archibald Lampman

A moment the wild swallows, like a flight
  Of withered gust-caught leaves, serenely high,
  Toss in the wind-rack up the muttering sky.
The leaves hang still. Above the weird twilight,
The hurrying centres of the storm unite
  And spreading with huge trunk and rolling fringe,
  Each wheeled upon its own tremendous hinge,
Tower darkening on. And now from heaven's height,
With the long roar of elm-trees swept and swayed,
  And pelted waters on the vanished plain
    Plunges the blast. Behind the wild white flash
    That splits abroad the pealing thunder-crash,
Over bleared fields and gardens disarrayed,
  Column on column comes the drenching rain.

Blue Suede Shoes
Words and Music by Carl Lee Perkins

Well, it's one for the money, two for the show,
three to get ready, now go, cat, go!
But don't you step on my BLUE SUEDE SHOES.
You can do anything but lay off my BLUE SUEDE SHOES.

Well, you can knock me down, step in my face,
slander my name all over the place;
Do anything that you want to do,
but uh-uh, honey, lay off of my shoes
Don't you step on my BLUE SUEDE SHOES.
You can do anything but lay off my BLUE SUEDE SHOES.

Burn my house, steal my car,
drink my cider from my old-fruit jar;
Do anything that you want to do,
but uh-uh, honey, lay off of my shoes
Don't you step on my BLUE SUEDE SHOES.
You can do anything but lay off my BLUE SUEDE SHOES.

BUILDING A WRITING CONTEXT

1. To what does the poet compare the machine in "Steam Shovel?" In keeping with this comparison, what does he say about its "head," "jaws," and "neck?"
2. In "Dreams" Langston Hughes compares life without dreams to a broken-winged bird. To what else does he compare it?
3. To what does Tennyson compare the eagle in the last line of the poem? What other comparison might a poet make involving an eagle? What do you notice about the rhyme pattern of this poem?
4. What words and phrases in "A Thunderstorm" help describe the power of the storm? What feelings are communicated in the poem?
5. If possible listen to a recording of "Blue Suede Shoes." What do you find unusual and interesting about the lyrics of this song?

THE WRITING WORKSHOP

Preparing to Write

A. Authors use comparisons and other kinds of figurative language to make language more precise, vigorous, and colourful. Figures of speech include:

- **Simile** — a comparison between two unlike things using *like, as,* or *than.* Example: "Like a thunderbolt he falls."

- **Metaphor** — a direct comparison between two unlike things without using *like, as,* or *than.* Example: "Life is a barren field."

- **Personification** — making things that are not human seem like people in some ways. Examples: "The road calls to me." "She made friends with the computer."

- **Hyperbole** — an intentionally exaggerated statement, used to show strong feeling. Examples: "He worked his fingers to the bone." "I'm so hungry I could eat a horse."

- **Understatement** — a purposely played-down statement; a form of sarcasm. Examples: "My leg is only broken in twelve places." "They call their tiny house The Mansion."

B. **Guidelines for Writing Lyric Poetry**
- Any story told in the poem is not as important as the experiences and feelings communicated.
- Use unusual or imaginative language to make the ordinary seem extraordinary. Figures of speech such as those listed above can be effective.
- You do not have to use a definite rhyme and rhythm pattern, but your lines should have a musical quality about them.

Developing the Writing

1. With a partner brainstorm topics or experiences of interest, and list them. Then develop a list of strong feelings. The lists below might help you get started. When your lists are completed, try to match items that seem to go together.

Topic/Experience/Idea	Strong Feeling
fullback	anger
baking a cake	joy
summer	amazement
storm	sorrow
taking out the garbage	wonder
oak tree	fear
whale	depression
	delight
_____	
_____	_____
_____	_____

2. Once you find a topic that is associated somehow for you with a strong feeling, brainstorm a list of words, phrases, and figures of speech that are somehow associated with this topic and feeling.
   Example:
     storm —————————— fear
   • Driving rain.
   • Trees snapped like toothpicks.
   • Waves are vicious paws.
   • Bridge out, radio dead.
   • Trees cry.
   • Blackened sky.
   • Not your basic sunshower.
   • Roar and rumble of thunder.
   • Flickering flashes of blinding light.
3. When you are happy with your list, start to organize it into a poem. Cross out, circle, number, underline, use arrows or any other symbols that will help you organize your random ideas into the beginnings of a structured poem.
4. Write your first draft.

Revising and Editing

1. Revise the first draft of your lyric poem by adding ideas, leaving out words, or re-organizing words and phrases. Here too cross out, circle, number, use arrows, or whatever is necessary to revise your draft into a better poem. Then write a second draft.

2. Edit your second draft in a group of four students. Use these questions:
   - Is the topic described in an unusual or interesting way?
   - Have figures of speech been used effectively?
   - Is the feeling or idea communicated in powerful and clear terms?
   - If there is a story in the poem, does it take second place to the experiences and feelings?
   - What ideas, words, or phrases should be added, left out, or reworded?

Sharing and Publishing

1. In groups of four take turns reading your lyric poems aloud. (Practise ahead of time.) After each reading the group should identify the topic of the poem read and discuss the experiences and feelings the writer is communicating. Effective use of vocabulary, rhyme, rhythm, and figures of speech should be highlighted and discussed.
2. Write your final draft in your best handwriting and take it home to share with members of your family. Keep the poem in your writing folder.

Growing from Writing

A. The poem "A Thunderstorm" comes alive when read orally. The punctuation marks in this poem give you clear directions on how to read it. Read it aloud several times, paying close attention to the punctuation. Continue reading it aloud until you are satisfied with your oral interpretation. You may also wish to try reading the poem aloud with a group of classmates.

B. Read "The Eagle" again, and then write a concise paragraph in which you describe how a squirrel, a whale, or a crayfish might view the world. For example, how would a canoe look to a crayfish? How would telephone wires look to a squirrel?

Advertisements

There's One Born Every Minute

You are surrounded by advertisements in newspapers and magazines, on television and radio, plastered on signs and billboards. How do you respond to an ad? What impact does advertising have on our culture?

There is greatness within every fish. But it takes genius to coax it out.

☑ Grouper   ☑ Tuna   ☑ Dover Sole   ☑ Sword Fish

☑ Lobster   ☑ Halibut   ☑ Red Snapper   ☐ Pompano

☑ Fillet of Sole   ☑ Blackened Redfish   ☑ Salmon   ☐ Trout

☑ Bay Scallops   ☑ Shrimp   ☑ Cold Shellfish Bouquet   ☐ Soft Shell ☑ Stone Crabs

Sample menu, November 25, 1985

The Manhattan Ocean Club The Poets of Fish.

West 58th Street, N.Y.C., between 5th and 6th Avenues. Open 7 days 'till midnight, 371-7777.

Lenox.

Rapunzel

An original, handcrafted work of art
intricately sculptured in fine porcelain…
individually painted by hand and
embellished with pure 24 karat gold.

Important first issue.
Available only by reservation.

For over 150 years, the story of the princess Rapunzel has touched our hearts and captured our imaginations, enchanting each generation anew with its romance, its fantasy, its beauty.

Now, inspired by the magic of Rapunzel's classic tale, Lenox has created an extraordinary new handpainted porcelain sculpture. In regal splendor, Rapunzel is captured in a delicate silk gown under a flowing robe of pastel blue velvet trimmed in ermine, edged with richly embroidered brocade, and

adorned with gleaming jewels. A floral tiara crowns her head and her hair is threaded with blue satin ribbons and strands of lustrous pearls.

**A Meticulously Handcrafted
Work of Art**

Conceived and designed by the artists of Lenox, *Rapunzel* is created exclusively under their direction by master craftsmen in Japan. Each figurine is crafted of fine bisque porcelain, capturing exqui-

BUSINESS REPLY MAIL

site detail from each flawlessly sculptured rose petal...to each individual pearl gracefully braided through her hair.

Skilled artisans paint each figurine *by hand,* evoking every subtle nuance of Rapunzel's beauty— from the faint blush of her cheek to the pale flaxen hues of her hair. *Pure 24 karat gold* is hand-applied to her necklace, hairbrush and jeweled accessories. And each figurine is embellished on its base in 24 karat gold with the title and the Lenox® trademark—symbol of uncompromising quality and craftsmanship.

Rapunzel is a triumph in the time-honored tradition of fine porcelain figurines, certain to be admired by all who see her. The intricate sculpting, with its wealth of fine detail, will be a source of enduring pleasure...the subtle blending of pastel tones will harmonize with any decor. And, like the classic tale that inspired her creation, *Rapunzel* will be cherished for generations to come.

Available Only Direct from Lenox

The important first issue in The Legendary Princesses by Lenox, *Rapunzel* is available only direct from Lenox and will not be sold through even the most prestigious dealers or galleries. The issue price is $114, payable in convenient monthly installments of $19 with *no finance charge.* Each figurine is accompanied by a Certificate of Authenticity and a story folder retelling her classic tale. And, of course, *your satisfaction is completely guaranteed.*

Since each figurine is individually handcrafted, please allow 8 to 10 weeks for delivery. Reservations are accepted in strict sequence of receipt and should be postmarked by March 31, 1986. To order, mail the reservation application. For your convenience on credit card orders, you may call **TOLL FREE,** 24 hours a day, 7 days a week, **1-800-228-5000.**

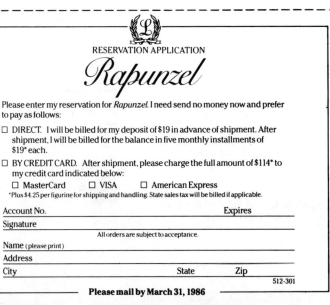

RESERVATION APPLICATION

Rapunzel

Please enter my reservation for *Rapunzel.* I need send no money now and prefer to pay as follows:

☐ DIRECT. I will be billed for my deposit of $19 in advance of shipment. After shipment, I will be billed for the balance in five monthly installments of $19* each.

☐ BY CREDIT CARD. After shipment, please charge the full amount of $114* to my credit card indicated below:

☐ MasterCard ☐ VISA ☐ American Express

*Plus $4.25 per figurine for shipping and handling. State sales tax will be billed if applicable.

Account No. _____ Expires _____

Signature _____

All orders are subject to acceptance.

Name (please print) _____

Address _____

City _____ State _____ Zip _____

512-301

Please mail by March 31, 1986

BUILDING A WRITING CONTEXT

1. At whom do you think each ad is aimed?
2. How successful is each approach, in your opinion?

3. What types of persuasion does each ad use?
4. What ads, if any, have influenced you strongly? In what ways?

THE WRITING WORKSHOP

Preparing to Write

Advertisements are not only effective in passing on information. They also form a sort of mirror of society, reflecting our culture's current concerns, trends, needs, and desires.

Though we tend to think of advertisements as ways of getting people to buy products, some advertisements have other messages. For example, a public service message might be about keeping the environment clean, taking care of the elderly, or caring for the disabled.

Developing the Writing

A. Look through a magazine or newspaper to find an advertisement that is not related to a product, but might be considered a public service message instead. Once you have found your advertisement, share it with a group of five or six classmates. As a group, discuss the following:
1. What immediately catches your attention in this advertisement?
2. Which are more effective in conveying a message — the words or the pictures?
3. Why was this advertisement created?
4. How does the advertisement make you react?
5. Is there too much information in the advertisement?
6. If the ad is in colour, has colour been effectively used?

B. Working individually or with a classmate, create an advertisement that would make others think about an issue of concern to our society. You may create a new advertisement on the same theme as one you have chosen from a magazine. Or you could choose a different message. Here are some suggestions:
- Preventing forest fires.
- Public transportation.
- Taking care of your health.
- Pollution.
- Education.

Once you have decided on a topic, consider the following questions:

1. What do I want the reader to think about?
2. How can I keep my wording simple?
3. How much space do I want my words to take up?
4. How will pictures help my message? (You may use magazine photos or real photos, or create your own drawings.)
5. What colours will best convey the mood of my advertisement?
6. How could my advertisement change someone else's behaviour?

Create your own advertisement.

Revising and Editing

Share your advertisement with a group. Imagine that it will be used for a billboard display throughout the country. Discuss as a group what changes need to be made in the advertisement. Especially consider how it might need to be adapted for billboard use.

Taking the other group members' suggestions into consideration, revise and edit your advertisement.

Sharing and Publishing

Display the final ads as a series of billboards in the hallway of your school.

Growing from Writing

A. People should obey certain rules of courtesy in movie theatres. Brainstorm a list of such rules. Then create a billboard poster that conveys one or more of your rules. (If you wish, substitute schools or restaurants for movie theatres.)

B. Create a billboard message using only words — no pictures. Limit your wording, creating a statement or asking a question that will catch people's attention. Examples:

• Have you hugged your child today?
• Careless drivers rest in pieces.
• Joe's Restaurant serves the best perogies in town.

The type of lettering, the colours you use, and the balance of blank space and text are just as important as the message you write.

C. You could try the same Activity as B above, using *only* pictures or diagrams to convey a message. No words allowed!

Opinion Articles — TV

Remaking Us in Its Own Image

There is growing evidence that television is not only influencing the life of the average Canadian; it is shaping it. It seems to be doing this not merely in its role as an exciting medium of news and entertainment, but as a whole environment; a one-way flow of sound and image — full of facts and reflections, interpretations, analyses, attitudes, and distortions — going directly into your home and thoughts every moment the set is turned on.

What important opinions about the effects of TV are reflected in the following article?

What TV Does to Kids

His first polysyllabic utterance was "Bradybunch." He learned to spell Sugar Smacks before his own name. Recently, he tried to karate-chop his younger sister after she broke his Six Million Dollar Man bionic transport station (she retaliated by bashing him with her Cher doll). His nursery-school teacher reports that he is passive, noncreative, and has almost no attention span; in short, he is very much like his classmates. This fall, he will officially reach the age of reason and begin his formal education. His parents are beginning to discuss their apprehensions — when they are not too busy watching television.

It is only in recent years — with the first TV generation already grown up — that social scientists, psychologists, pediatricians and educators have begun serious study of the impact of television on the young. According to television survey-taker A.C. Nielsen, children under five watch an average of 23.5 hours of TV a week. Today's typical high-school graduate has logged at least 15,000 hours before the small screen — more time than he has spent on any other activity except sleep. At present levels of advertising and mayhem, he will have been exposed to 350,000 commercials and vicariously participated in 18,000 killings. The conclusion is inescapable: After parents, television has become perhaps the most potent influence on the beliefs, values and behavior of the young.

Unquestionably, the plug-in picture window has transmitted some benefits. In general, the children of TV enjoy a more sophisticated knowledge of a far larger world. They are likely to possess richer vocabularies, albeit with only a superficial comprehension of what the words mean. Research on the impact of "Sesame Street" has established measurable gains in the cognitive skills of many pre-schoolers.

Nonetheless, the overwhelming body of evidence — drawn from more than 2,300 studies and reports — is decidedly negative. Michael Rothenberg, a child psychiatrist at the University of Washington, has reviewed the 50 most compre-hensive studies involving 10,000 children from every possible background. Most showed that viewing violence tends to produce aggressive behavior among the young. "The time is long past due for a major, organized cry of protest from the medical profession," concludes Rothenberg.

An unexpected salvo was sounded last winter when the normally cautious American Medical Association asked ten major corporations to review their policies about sponsoring excessively gory shows. "TV violence is both a mental-health problem and an environmental issue," explained Dr. Richard E. Palmer, president of the AMA. In defense, broadcasting officials maintain that the jury is still out on whether video violence is guilty of producing aggressive behavior. And network schedulers say they are actively reducing the violence dosage.

But televised mayhem is only part of TV's impact. TV has at the very least preempted the traditional development of childhood itself. The time kids spend sitting catatonic before the set has been exacted from such salutary pursuits as reading, outdoor play, even simple, contemplative solitude. Few parents

can cope with its tyrannical allure. Recently, Dr. Benjamin
Spock took his stepdaughter and granddaughter to New York to
see a concert and a Broadway show. But the man who has the
prescription for everything from diaper rash to bedwetting had
no easy solution for dislodging the kids from their hotel room.
"Of all the attractions in New York," recalls Spock, "they
seemed to find the TV set the most fascinating."

Small wonder that television has been called "the flickering
blue parent." The after-school and early-evening hours used to
be a time for "what-did-you-do-today" dialogue. Now, the
electronic box does most of the talking. Dr. David Pearl of the
U.S. National Institute of Mental Health suspects that the tube
"has displaced many of the normal interactional processes
between parents and children which are essential for maximum
development."

Even more worrisome is what television has done to, rather
than denied, the tube-weaned population. A series of studies has
shown that addiction to TV stifles creative imagination. For
example, a University of Southern California research team
exposed 250 elementary students to three weeks of intensive
viewing. Tests found a marked drop in all forms of creative
abilities except verbal skill. Some teachers are encountering
children who cannot understand a simple story without visual
illustrations. Nursery-school teachers who have observed the
pre-TV generation contend that juvenile play is far less
imaginative and spontaneous than in the past. "You don't see
kids making their own toys out of crummy things like we used
to," says University of Virginia psychology professor Stephen
Worchel. "You don't see them playing hopscotch, or making up
their own games. Everything is suggested to them by
television."

Too much TV too early may also instill an attitude of
spectatorship, a withdrawal from direct involvement in real-life
experiences. "What television basically teaches children is
passivity," says Stanford University researcher Paul Kaufman.
"It creates the illusion of having been somewhere and done
something and seen something, when in fact they've been sitting
at home."

Conditioned to see all problems resolved in 30 or 60 minutes,
the offspring of TV exhibit a low tolerance for the frustration of
learning. Grade-schoolers are quickly turned off by any activity

that promises less than instant gratification. "You introduce a new skill, and right away, if it looks hard, they dissolve into tears," laments one first-grade teacher. "They want everything to be easy — like watching the tube."

The debate over the link between TV violence and aggressive behavior in society has had a longer run than "Gunsmoke." Today, however, even zealous network apologists concede that some children, under certain conditions, will imitate antisocial acts seen on the tube. Indeed a study of 100 juvenile offenders commissioned by ABC found that no fewer than 22 confessed to having copied criminal techniques from TV. Behavioral sleuths are also uncovering evidence that the tide of TV carnage increases children's tolerance of violent behavior in others, because they have been conditioned to think of violence as an everyday thing. . . .

A few daring parents have counterattacked by simply pulling the plug. Charles Frye, a San Francisco nursery-school teacher and the father of five boys, decided he would not replace his set after it conked out. . . . Frye's brood rebelled at first, but today 14-year-old Mark fills his afternoon hours with tapdancing lessons, scout meetings and work in a gas station. Kirk, his 13-year-old brother, plays a lot of basketball and football and recently finished *Watership Down* and all four of the Tolkien hobbit books.

Short of such a draconian measure, some parents are exercising a greater degree of home rule. Two years ago, the administrators of New York's Horace Mann nursery school became distressed over an upsurge of violence in their students' play. Deciding that television was to blame, they dispatched a letter to all parents urging them to curb their children's viewing. "After we sent the letter, we could see a change," recalls principal Eleanor Brussel. "The kids showed better concentration, better comprehension, an ability to think things through."

Clearly, there is no single antidote. For the children of today, and their progeny to come, TV watching will continue to be their most shared — and shaping — experience. Virtually all the experts agree, however, on one palliative. Instead of using TV as an electronic babysitter, parents must try to involve themselves directly in their youngsters' viewing. By watching along with the kids at least occasionally, they can help them evaluate what they see — pointing out the inflated claims of a commercial, perhaps, or criticizing a gratuitously violent scene. "Parents don't have to regard TV as a person who can't be interrupted," says behavioral scientist Charles Corder-Bolz. "If they view one show a night with their kids, and make just one or two comments about it, they can have more impact than the whole program."

Reduced to the essentials, the question for parents no longer is: "Do you know where your children are tonight?" The question has become: "What are they watching — and with whom?"

BUILDING A WRITING CONTEXT

1. **Try switching the order of the first and second paragraphs? What is the effect? Why do you think the author put the first paragraph first?**
2. **Why does the author use statistics in the second paragraph? What is their effect on the reader?**
3. **In what way do the last four paragraphs of the article differ from the earlier ones? Why do you think the author chose to conclude the article in this way?**

THE WRITING WORKSHOP

Preparing to Write

The opinion article "What TV Does to Kids" includes the following main parts:

1. A "lead" paragraph to attract the reader's attention and make him or her want to go on reading. In this case it is a description of a particular child affected by TV. Other types of "leads" include: a personal experience, a joke, a quotation, a startling fact, a little story.
2. A statement of the article's main ideas: second paragraph.
3. Several paragraphs expanding on these main ideas.
4. Conclusion: last four paragraphs.

Developing the Writing

The article "What TV Does to Kids" deals mainly with television's effects on young children. Write an article in which

110

you give your opinions of TV's effects on teenagers. In your article include the four main parts listed above. Your article may be mainly in favour of TV; it may be mainly opposed; or it may try to provide a balanced viewpoint somewhere in the middle. The following lists of points may help you get started.

- **Points in favour of TV**
  1. Nobody's forced to watch TV — if you don't like it, switch it off!
  2. We are still free to enjoy "cultural" things.
  3. Only when there is a lack of moderation can TV be bad. (This is true for many things in life.)
  4. If you boast that you don't watch TV, it's like boasting that you don't read books. We have to watch TV to be well-informed.
  5. There is a considerable variety of programs; we can select what we want to see.
  6. TV is a continuous cheap source of information and entertainment.
  7. TV has enormous possibilities for education.
  8. TV provides education in its broadest sense: ideals of democracy, politics, controversial issues.
  9. TV provides many people — such as the actors, broadcasters, and producers — with employment and an outlet for their creative abilities.
  10. TV is a unifying force in the world.

- **Points against TV**
  1. Because of TV, some people are losing interest in hobbies, entertaining others, outside activities, and so on.
  2. People used to read more books, listen to more music, talk more with friends.
  3. Many people's free time now seems to be regulated by TV.
  4. TV viewing demands silence; people are afraid to upset viewers, so are reluctant to communicate.
  5. Whole generations are growing up addicted; people are neglecting other things.
  6. TV plays the role of a member of the family.
  7. Young people are exposed to and influenced by the sex and violence, simplistic programs, distorted values, trendy

morality, rubbishy commercials — hours spent in mindless
viewing.
8. Our society is becoming illiterate, dependent on pictures
and words. The written language almost seems unnecessary.
9. TV encourages passive enjoyment; second-hand
experience.
10. TV cuts us off from the day-to-day "real" world.

Revising and Editing

When you wrote the first draft of your television opinion article,
you were probably most interested in organizing the information
in sentences and paragraphs. It is only natural — when
concentrating on content and organization — to make
mechanical errors in spelling, punctuation, capitalization, and
grammar. Thus, it is now very important that you read through
your first draft carefully, looking for such errors. Correct any
errors you find.

Sharing and Publishing

Exchange articles with two or more classmates. Read each
other's articles. Try to read at least one article that expresses
opinions quite different from your own.

Growing from Writing

Have a classroom debate on the resolution: "Movies should be
censored."
The following lists of points will help you start thinking about
this topic.

- **Pro**
  1. Adults have a responsibility to protect young people from
     what they consider to be undesirable influences.
  2. If young people need protection, so do adults.
  3. Not all adults are mature enough to decide what's good for
     them.
  4. Like the law, censorship is good for society as a whole.
  5. Censors are extremely open-minded — they clearly
     recognize artistic merit.
  6. When censorship laws are relaxed, unscrupulous people are

given a licence to produce virtually anything in the name of ''art.''

7. Without censorship, some producers would be free to corrupt the minds of viewers.

8. To argue in favour of absolute freedom is to argue in favour of anarchy.

- **Con**

  1. Whether or not there is censorship, careful parents would still be in a position to protect young people from movies they wouldn't want them to see.

  2. Censorship is dangerous in that it limits and controls the way people feel and think.

  3. In totalitarian countries like Russia, censorship has led to absolute control by the state.

  4. Censorship is not consistent with the ideas of democracy: for example, freedom of expression.

  5. There is no such thing as an all-wise human being — who then shall be the censor?

  6. History shows that there have been many idiotic decisions made by ''protectors of the public.''

  7. Banning movies or parts of movies has the effect of drawing attention to them.

Essays

Give Me a Ballpark Figure

Human imagination is important. Our imaginations helped us get from the Stone Age to the Space Age. Our imaginations can help us solve problems facing the world today. Pollution, family matters, health, urban planning, education, peace, food, race relations, transportation — imagination and flexible thinking can help find solutions.

Computers have no imagination or flexibility of thought — right? To a computer, everything is always true or false, black or white. Perhaps this has been so in the past. But as the following essay explains, computers may soon be capable of much more flexible thinking.

"Fuzzy" Math Is More Human

Professor Madan Gupta, of the Cybernetics Research Laboratory, University of Saskatchewan College of Engineering, is one of the pioneers of a relatively new branch of mathematics aimed at creating "intelligent" machines and control systems. Called "fuzzy arithmetic," it is based on approximate as distinct from precise reasoning. As a result, it may enable machines to perform complex and subtle tasks that presently can be done only by humans.

Professor Gupta pointed out that computer programming rooted in conventional mathematics is very rigid and precise. This is because the classical logic at the basis of the mathematics has only two values, true or false (or one and zero when expressed arithmetically). In such a system all classes (sets) are assumed to have sharply defined boundaries, so that objects or numbers either belong to the class or set, or do not belong.

This works fine when dealing with clear alternatives like life or death, or distinct commands like start and stop in the control of industrial processes. However, in the real world and in human thinking most classes have imprecise or "fuzzy" boundaries, and there are degrees of membership. A person, for example, may be more or less tall, an industrial process may require more or less heat depending on a host of variables that are themselves imprecise.

Professor Gupta said it is the ability of humans to think in fuzzy terms that enables them to understand, for instance, an almost infinite variety of handwriting and to control complex chemical processes by rules of thumb. With handwriting, they know what particular letters are "more or less" supposed to look like, and can recognize even distorted versions. Computers, on the other hand, will consider the same letters to be different unless they are similar in a rigidly prescribed sense.

Fuzzy arithmetic was conceived in the mid-1960s to translate imprecise or approximate reasoning into numerical terms that computers can use. The way computers do this is through fuzzy sets (classes) in which there are various degrees of membership. Fuzzy concepts like "small," "low," "slightly," "usually," and "most" can be given numerical values that express this membership. In a chemical plant, for example, a temperature of 1000 degrees might be defined in the computer program as having a 0.9 membership in the set of high temperatures. A temperature of 500 degrees, however, might be given only a 0.4 degree of membership.

Professor Gupta noted that the first major commercial application of fuzzy logic has been in the control of chemical processes. The variables are so complex and imprecise that they defy conventional mathematics. People, however, can monitor them using approximate rules of thumb.

BUILDING A WRITING CONTEXT

1. **The first paragraph presents the main idea of the essay. State this main idea in your own words.**

2. In the second, third, and fourth paragraphs, the author develops the main idea by using comparison. What does the author compare? Why?
3. Why do you think the author keeps using the word *fuzzy*? How might the effect have been different if the word *flexible* had been used instead?
4. What is the author's purpose in the last two paragraphs?

THE WRITING WORKSHOP

Preparing to Write

An essay is not meant to be a presentation of everything you know about a subject. Rather, it should be a carefully organized and well-written exploration of one main idea.

Every essay writer approaches the task in a somewhat different way. You must find an approach that works for you, and for the particular type of essay you are writing. You may find the following steps useful, especially for essays containing a good deal of factual material.

1. Select a topic.
2. Formulate a series of questions about the topic. The questions should not just yield yes/no answers, but should be designed to elicit more detailed information.
3. Try to answer your own questions, using outside resources if necessary.
4. Summarize your ideas and findings.
5. Draw a generalization from your summary. This may serve as the main idea, or thesis, of your essay.
6. Write an essay setting forth your ideas and findings. If appropriate, cite evidence from outside resources to support your position.

Developing the Writing

A. Revise the following thesis statements, writing a more complete and interesting statement in each case.
• Example: The first week of school was quite an experience.
• Revision: The first week of school was a long series of frustrations, from my arrival in general assembly to my last class.

1. Robert Redford's (or any movie star's) movies are exciting.
   Revision:
2. Participation in school sports builds character.
   Revision:
3. Barbecuing hamburgers is an art.
   Revision:
4. Christmas has become too commercialized.
   Revision:
5. Cold weather is an inconvenience.
   Revision:
6. Physical fitness is important.
   Revision:

B. Select one of the following topics and write a "skeleton" essay, containing the following: an introductory paragraph ending with a thesis (main idea) statement, topic sentences for each of three paragraphs within the essay, and a concluding paragraph.
1. The threat of Communism.
2. Why vote?
3. The tyranny of the automobile.
4. How to improve our school.
5. Child abuse.
6. Divorce.
7. Escapes from reality.
8. What it takes to be successful.

C. Develop a complete essay based on your "skeleton" essay in Activity B.

D. In a small group, brainstorm the following topics. Then each member of the group should select one topic for individual exploration. Discuss your topic with your group and jot down any worthwhile ideas. Then write a personal essay on your topic.
1. An adventure in friendship.
2. The virtues of idleness.
3. Pages from my family history.
4. Being contented.
5. Crushes and hero-worship.
6. The most valuable thing I have learned.
7. An important decision.

8. Let me cry on your shoulder.
9. Worrying is good for you.
10. Going around in circles.

Revising and Editing

Use the following questions to evaluate your essay. Make any improvements you can.
1. Is there a clear pattern by which I develop my thesis, or main idea?
2. Does each paragraph fit into this pattern and advance my thesis?
3. Does my introduction give a clear idea of what the essay is about?
4. Are there problems of emphasis? Do I give proper stress to my most important idea?
5. Are my points presented in the proper order?
6. Do I use effective transitions, both to unify paragraphs and to connect them to one another?
7. Does my essay have a forceful ending?

Growing from Writing

A. Many essays are written about people and their deeds. Usually the type of people portrayed in essays are men and women of strength and substance — stubborn, confident people, who hold to their convictions with courage and tenacity.

Identify some person whom you admire because he or she has taken a firm stand on some issue and supported it in the face of strong opposition. You could choose as a subject someone you know personally, or a public figure. Write an essay characterizing this person and explain what it is you admire in him or her.

B. Write a defence of some idea that you have proposed without success, but that you still feel is valid. The cause you support should be one that is generally unpopular. (You may, if you like, treat this essay humorously, inventing a cause that is obviously indefensible and defending it with mock seriousness.)

Observation

Milk River Mystery

People have always had a strong desire to leave records of their activities. These records — whether chiselled in stone, baked on clay tablets, written on parchment, or fed into a computer — give us a picture of how people lived. Such writings reveal the life and culture of the past. Whether records were written yesterday or thousands of years ago, they are useful in helping us understand the world in which we live today.

Canada doesn't have the long written history of Europe or Asia. Our written history is relatively short, particularly that of western Canada. Following is an account of one intriguing piece of western Canadian history — that of the mysterious stone-age writing in the Milk River Valley of Alberta.

Writing-On-Stone   ALICE A. CAMPBELL

This land of stone-age writing lies in the Milk River Valley about twenty miles (32 km) east of Milk River. It is known as Masinasin, the Indian name which means Writing-On-Stone. Before the last war, the provincial government realizing that there was a need to preserve the hieroglyphic stones and the strange obelisks, turned the area into a provincial park on August 31, 1935. . . .

Most of the writings on the rocks lie a little distance to the west of the picnic grounds but a road has been built that circles the area of the writings. . . . there are many places along the river where writings on the sandstone rocks are found. . . .

Major Fred Bagley in his story "The '71 Mounties" tells of seeing Indian pictographs painted on the rocks and caves near their camp in the Sweet Grass Hills. This was probably at the place later known as Writing-On-Stone and also opposite the mouth of what is called Police Coulee. He states that one group of paintings represented a battle and another told of a buffalo hunt.

Major Bagley tells a legend concerning Writing-On-Stone. A group of Indians set out on a buffalo hunt. They were successful in the chase but were overtaken by a fierce blizzard. Taking shelter below the rocks, they painted the story of the hunt but all perished before the storm abated.

At one point there is pictured the surrounding scene of a background of the Sweet Grass Hills, the high cliffs, the river and symbols representing people in action. Evidently it was the record of an event that took place at that point.

Most of the writings are petroglyphs, as they are carved in the rock. Some of the rocks with writing on them have fallen during the past few years, due to erosion, and the writing is lost. The faces of some of the harder rocks have been painted with a pigment, red in color, which is very like the pigment found at the Paint Pots at Marble Canyon. Many writings have been defaced by people cutting initials in them and trying to fake the writing.

There is a legend that Indians believe the writing changes every night and that it has a new meaning each morning. One scene pictures a woman skipping with a skipping rope. The rope was likely a clematis vine. These vines grow around the rocks. They are thick, long and very tough. This skipping incident may have been an endurance test. The early Indians are said to have held war games and feats of strength on the flats where they would camp.

The writings are mostly in groups, each group telling a story. One group, present-day Indians say, tells the story of two braves who were brothers. They had been trying desperately to obtain food for their people. It was a year of famine, as the buffalo had gone elsewhere to better feeding grounds. Then one day a herd of buffalo was sighted. The brothers hurried to get what meat they could. In the herd they spied one fat buffalo. The brothers each marked it for his own. When it fell, both brothers claimed having made the kill, as both arrows had found a vital spot.

Enraged at each other, they fought until both dropped dead. That drama is vividly pictured on the rock.

Many leading archaeologists have visited the rocks and studied the writings. They conclude that the region had been visited by a race of people who were intelligent and were here before the Indians. It is known that an earlier race passed through the province, as tools and pottery have been found that were used by an earlier people. Various types of flint arrow heads, sharp-edged scrapers and many kinds of hammer heads have been found around the Milk River area.

Professor J.W.T. Spinks, in charge of exploration by a party from the University of Saskatchewan, found traces of prehistoric-man of the Yuma Culture forty miles (64 km) south-east of Saskatoon. Bearers of the Yuma Culture are believed to have inhabited Arizona and Mexico, but there are indications that they were driven further north. Perhaps they left the hieroglyphic writing on the rocks of the Milk River.

Others think that perhaps the Malayo-Polynesians drifted across the Pacific to British Columbia about the end of the first millenium A.D. The French anthropologist Mauss and Professor A.L. Krober are among those who think there was some such migration instead of over the roof of the world from Asia. Thor Heyerdahl, Norwegian scientist, advanced the most challenging evidence in 1940, that remnants of some South Sea culture reached the Bella Coola Valley many ages ago. His research led him to conclude that these advanced people were driven from the Bella Coola Valley by the war-like Salish Indians of the lower Fraser Valley, three hundred miles (483 km) farther south. It may be possible that these people found a pass across the mountains and followed the winding rivers over the prairies. These barren lands would offer no means of a livelihood. Perhaps it is they who left the record of their wanderings.

BUILDING A WRITING CONTEXT

1. In your opinion, when does something become historically important? In other words, how old does something have to be before it becomes a "site" or "monument?"

2. Why is it important to make areas of land such as that described here into provincial or national parks? What

might be the difference if commercial companies bought the land?

3. Some archeologists believe the petroglyphs could be Malayo-Polynesian in origin. How probable do you think this explanation is?

THE WRITING WORKSHOP

Preparing to Write

After you know a subject well as a writer, you commit yourself to presenting your thoughts clearly to an audience. If your material is exciting and clear to you, chances are it will appear forceful and clear to the reader.

Most of us go through each day looking for what we saw yesterday and we find it, to our disappointment. In a sense, all our todays become dull yesterdays. But the person who daily expects to encounter the unique features of everyday realities will run smack into them again and again. People such as these keep their minds and eyes open.

Developing the Writing

A. Keep a piece of paper or a notebook in your pocket for two days, and jot down five unique features of everyday life that you see around you. When you come home, write them in sentences. Then revise and tighten your sentences. Consider building up to the surprises, rather than giving them away early in your statements. Example:

Like rather shabby soldiers standing guard between the two yards is a row of fence posts, which are regularly visited by robins.

B. "There is a legend that Indians believe the writing changes every night and that it has a new meaning each morning." *Alice A. Campbell*

This quote from the article may inspire us to take a fresh look at life every day, searching for new levels of meaning. Choose one of the following topics. Write two paragraphs about that topic, expressing a different meaning in each paragraph. For example, if you are writing about "the most beautiful spot I know,'' you could write about what it meant to you when you first saw it, and then about what it meant to you when you shared it with someone you love.

1. The most beautiful spot I know.
2. A sunset.
3. Spring in the country.
4. A crowded restaurant.
5. Interior of an old-fashioned shop (e.g., shoe repair shop, barber shop, music store, butcher shop).
6. A lonesome road.
7. School sounds.
8. A street scene.
9. A mysterious sound.

C. Pretend you are a person who made some of the petroglyphs in the Milk River Valley. Write two or more paragraphs to tell about it. Be sure to explain who you are and why you made the petroglyphs.

Revising and Editing

Reread your writing, revising it as necessary according to the revision checklist on page 144.

Sharing and Publishing

Put your writing in your writing folder. Later you may wish to use it as part of a longer piece of writing.

Growing from Writing

A. To find out more about petroglyphs, refer to the following or similar books:
• *Indian Petroglyphs* by Beth and Ray Hill (Hancock House).
• *Indian Rock Paintings of the Great Lakes* by Selwyn Dewdney (University of Toronto Press).

B. Draw a modern petroglyph showing some particularly meaningful event in your life.

Projects

What Ever Happened to the Sabre-toothed Tiger?

Too much hunting by Stone Age people may have helped bring about the extinction of the sabre-toothed tiger and other huge prehistoric animals like the mammoth. Later, when guns became common, tens of millions of animals were killed for food, for their skins, and just for "sport."

Wild animals on some islands have been killed off, not by people directly, but by domesticated animals brought to the islands by people. And millions of animals are killed each year because they prey on people's domestic animals or damage crops.

Today, however, the greatest single danger to wildlife is probably the destruction of wild places. Throughout the world, forests are being cleared to make way for farms to help feed hungry people. Rivers are being diverted and polluted, and cities are spreading. Everywhere, as "civilization" spreads, wildlife is driven back. Read the following article about an animal that once faced extinction but, because of careful planning, has made a comeback in recent decades.

The Effort to Save Animals JOHN BURTON

Many animals are on the verge of extinction today. There are many reasons why this is so, and there are usually reasons why a particular animal is in danger. Some animals have decreased in number for hundreds of years due to changes in climate and vegetation. For instance, the giant panda and the whooping crane are both rare, probably for these reasons. Other animals, such as the North American bison and the Arabian oryx, are rare because of senseless and destructive hunting. But probably most endangered animals are threatened because of people's intrusion in the places in which they live.

When the first settlers were moving across America's "Wild West," the herds of bison (or buffalo, as they are sometimes called) seemed limitless. There were probably sixty million bison roaming the plains in herds that often contained several thousand animals. As the settlers spread across the prairies, so the hunters went ahead. Sometimes they were employed to supply meat for workmen on the railroads, but often the slaughter was far greater than was needed to supply their needs. At that time it seemed that the bison would last forever — but by the beginning of this century there were only a few hundred left throughout America. By careful conservation, people have now managed to re-establish several large herds, and in the National Parks of Canada and the U.S.A. these magnificent animals can once more be seen.

Few people realize that a bison very similar to the one found in America once roamed Europe. The European bison, or wisent, lived mainly in deep forests. As the forests were cut down, so the bison were hunted and exterminated. By the beginning of the twentieth century, they existed only deep in the forest of Bialowieza, in Poland. They were fairly safe there until World War I, when a shortage of food led to the slaughter of the last 737. Luckily, there were several zoos, and after the war as many bison as possible were gathered together in an enclosure in the Bialowieza Forest and allowed to breed. In 1956 some were allowed to roam wild, and since then small herds have been released in remote forests in Russia and Romania.

BUILDING A WRITING CONTEXT

1. Do you mind whether or not tinned food for pet cats and dogs contains whale meat? Would you buy it if you knew it contained such meat, and if you thought the whales were being threatened?
2. Do you think it is a good idea to farm wild animals, like the buffalo and caribou, for food? Would you eat them?
3. What are some arguments for and against hunting and shooting such animals as foxes, deer, tigers, and elephants?
4. What distinction would you make between hunting for trophies such as lion skins or deer antlers, and hunting for food?
5. How do you think it is possible to preserve wildlife in the face of economic pressures, and growing needs for industrial development and agricultural land?

THE WRITING WORKSHOP

Preparing to Write

If a writing topic is assigned and the writer at first feels he or she has little to say about it, he or she must mentally turn it over and over, coming at it from many angles. The writer must keep turning the subject over mentally until he or she finds a place where some aspect of the subject intersects with his or her past experiences and/or present interests.

This is why journalists and reporters often talk of "finding an angle." They may be asked to write about a certain topic, but at first not know how to begin. However, once they find a point at which they personally intersect with a subject, they are on their way. Often the starting point suggests the whole direction of the article.

Developing the Writing

Use one of the following sets of questions and answers as the basis for an article. One "angle" is suggested for each. Either use this angle. Or, after turning the topic over in your mind, come up with an angle of your own. Do research as necessary in order to develop your article.

1. Question: There are still over 4000 species of mammals, and over eight and a half thousand species of birds. The number of species lost does not amount to much more than 1%. There are birds and animals everywhere. How can it be argued that wildlife is in danger?

   Answer: About 120 species of mammals and nearly 200 of birds are on the danger list, along with many sub-species. Many more are extinct locally; others are extremely rare; and many are greatly reduced in numbers. The future of all the larger mammals (especially the large cats) is threatened.

   Possible Angle: My cat lives the "life of Reilly." Few dangers threaten him. But what about his wild relatives?

2. Question: Hunting and shooting are great fun. Shooting is truly exciting and worth any amount of watching wildlife on TV. Aren't conservationists just poor sports trying to put an end to pleasure?

   Answer: If hunting continues as it has, there will soon be nothing left to hunt. If wildlife is managed properly, it may be possible both to retain breeding numbers and allow shooting and hunting — although many conservationists would oppose killing simply for fun.

   Possible Angle: My aunt and uncle make their living as hunting guides. Yet they also consider themselves serious conservationists. How can this be, you ask?

3. Question: Millions of people in the world today are starving. We have not yet learned how to feed all the people alive today. Is it fair to put land aside for animals, and grow food for them, when millions of people are going hungry?

   Answer: Properly managed, wildlife can add to the food supply of the world and can yield valuable protein. Wildlife can be a resource, not a liability, provided that numbers for breeding are kept up.

   Possible Angle: I ate delicious "buffalo burgers" at the fair. Bison (buffalo) meat is of excellent quality. These once-endangered animals have made such a comeback that they are now being ranched, and may become an important food source in the future.

4. Question: Is it right to spend money on nature conservation, when people have so many problems? Surely the money should be put into something of direct value to people, such as cancer research.

Answer: Conservation and cancer research are not alternatives; we should do both. Neither costs a fraction of what is spent on preparations for war, or on sending people into space, or even on smoking or gambling. Far more money is spent on cats and dogs than on wild animals.

Possible Angle: His Royal Highness Prince Philip has for many years been known for his work in wildlife conservation. Wildlife organizations in which Canadian students could participate include: World Wildlife Fund, Canadian Wildlife Federation, Ducks Unlimited, and Canadian Wolf Defenders.

Revising and Editing

As you reread your article, look for possible improvements you could make, using the following questions as a guide.
1. Active Voice: Is my article dominated by strong, active constructions, rather than by weak, passive constructions?
2. Development: Are details sufficient in number? Are details, especially the most significant ones, developed fully enough?
3. Emphasis: Where does the main emphasis lie? Is it clear?
4. Originality: Does my sentence structure vary for the sake of interest and emphasis? Are the details presented in a fresh, striking way?
5. Diction: Have I chosen specific, concrete words wherever possible, rather than abstract, general ones?

Sharing and Publishing

Consider submitting the final draft of your article to a school newspaper, a community newspaper, or some other periodical.

Growing from Writing

Make a poster that relates in some way to the general theme "Together We Can Help Wildlife." Keep the following guidelines in mind.

1. Demonstrate understanding of the theme and effectively communicate that theme.
2. Be accurate in your presentation of wildlife. (For example, there should be no tigers pouncing on Rocky Mountain crocodiles!)
3. Use any artistic medium you wish; for example: paint, felt pen, charcoals, photography, collage, batik. You could even consider mixing media.
4. The words of the theme or other phrases relevant to the theme may be used, but are not absolutely necessary as long as the meaning is clear.

Writing about Literature

Lieutenant Blandford's Rose

The "literary paper" — the paragraph or essay that deals with some aspect or aspects of a work of literature — is a familiar assignment to most students. Such an assignment develops your skill both as a reader and as a writer. The range of subjects that literary papers cover is as broad as literature itself. You may be asked, for example, to interpret a poem, to analyze the role of a particular character in a novel, or to make judgments on the effectiveness of a short story writer's style.

As you read the following short story, start to think about how you would comment on it.

Appointment with Love S.I. KISHOR

Six minutes to six, said the great round clock over the information booth in Grand Central Station. The tall young Army lieutenant who had just come from the direction of the tracks lifted his sunburned face, and his eyes narrowed to note the exact time. His heart was pounding with a beat that shocked him because he could not control it. In six minutes, he would see the woman who had filled such a special place in his life for the past thirteen months, the woman he had never seen, yet whose written words had been with him and sustained him unfailingly.

He placed himself as close as he could to the information booth, just beyond the ring of people besieging the clerks. . . .

Lieutenant Blandford remembered one night in particular, the worst of the fighting, when his plane had been caught in the midst of a pack of Zeros. He had seen the grinning face of one of the enemy pilots.

In one of his letters, he had confessed to her that he often felt fear, and only a few days before this battle, he had received her answer: "Of course you fear . . . all brave men do. Didn't King David know fear? That's why he wrote the Twenty-third Psalm. Next time you doubt yourself, I want you to hear my voice reciting to you: 'Yea, though I walk through the valley of the shadow of death, I shall fear no evil, for Thou art with me'. . ." And he had remembered; he had heard her imagined voice, and it had renewed his strength and skill.

Now he was going to hear her real voice. Four minutes to six. His face grew sharp.

Under the immense, starred roof, people were walking fast, like threads of color being woven into a gray web. A girl passed close to him, and Lieutenant Blandford started. She was wearing a red flower in her suit lapel, but it was a crimson sweet pea, not the little red rose they had agreed upon. Besides, this girl was too young, about eighteen whereas Hollis Meynell had frankly told him she was thirty. "Well, what of it?" he had answered. "I'm thirty-two." He was twenty-nine.

His mind went back to that book — the book the Lord Himself must have put into his hands out of the hundreds of Army library books sent to the Florida training camp. *Of Human Bondage*, it was; and throughout the book were notes in a woman's writing. He had always hated that writing-in habit, but these remarks were different. He had never believed that a woman could see into a man's heart so tenderly, so understandingly. Her name was on the bookplate: Hollis Meynell. He had got hold of a New York City telephone book and found her address. He had written, she had answered. Next day he had been shipped out, but they had gone on writing.

For thirteen months, she had faithfully replied, and more than replied. When his letters did not arrive, she wrote anyway, and now he believed he loved her, and she loved him.

But she had refused all his pleas to send him her photograph. That seemed rather bad, of course. But she had explained: "If your feeling for me has any reality, any honest basis, what I look like won't matter. Suppose I'm beautiful. I'd always be haunted by the feeling that you had been taking a chance on just that, and that kind of love would disgust me. Suppose I'm plain (and you must admit that this is more likely) then I'd always fear that you were going on writing to me only because you were lonely and had no one else. No, don't ask for my picture. When you come to New York, you shall see me and then you shall make your decision. Remember, both of us are free to stop or to go on after that — whichever we choose. . . ."

One minute to six . . . he pulled hard on a cigarette.

Then Lieutenant Blandford's heart leaped higher than his plane had ever done.

A young woman was coming toward him. Her figure was long and slim; her blond hair lay back in curls from her delicate ears. Her eyes were blue as flowers, her lips and chin had a gentle firmness. In her pale green suit, she was like springtime come alive.

He started toward her, entirely forgetting to notice that she was wearing no rose, and as he moved, a small, provocative smile curved her lips.

"Going my way, soldier?" she murmured.

Uncontrollably, he made one step closer to her. Then he saw Hollis Meynell.

She was standing almost directly behind the girl, a woman well past forty, her graying hair tucked under a worn hat. She was more than plump; her thick ankled feet were thrust into low-heeled shoes. But she wore a red rose in the rumpled lapel of her brown coat.

The girl in the green suit was walking quickly away.

Blandford felt as though he were being split in two, so keen was his desire to follow the girl, yet so deep was his longing for the woman whose spirit had truly companioned and upheld his own; and there she stood. Her pale, plump face was gentle and sensible; he could see that now. Her gray eyes had a warm, kindly twinkle.

Lieutenant Blandford did not hesitate. His fingers gripped the small, worn, blue leather copy of *Of Human Bondage* which was to identify him to her. This would not be love, but it would be something precious, something perhaps even rarer than love — a friendship for which he had been and must ever be grateful. . . .

He squared his broad shoulders, saluted and held the book out
toward the woman, although even while he spoke he felt
choked by the bitterness of his disappointment.

"I'm Lieutenant John Blandford, and you — you are Miss
Meynell. I'm so glad you could meet me. May — may I take
you to dinner?"

The woman's face broadened in a tolerant smile. "I don't
know what this is all about, son," she answered. "That young
lady in the green suit — the one who just went by — begged me
to wear this rose on my coat. And she said that if you asked me
to go out with you, I should tell you that she's waiting for you
in that big restaurant across the street. She said it was some
kind of a test. I've got two boys with Uncle Sam myself, so I
didn't mind to oblige you."

BUILDING A WRITING CONTEXT

1. **How is suspense created at the beginning of the story?**
2. **How and why does the author use flashback?**
3. **What is the emotional impact of the ending?**

THE WRITING WORKSHOP

Preparing to Write

In writing about what you have read in books, you should try to
speak in a voice that rings true and strikes the ear hard. Don't
generalize. Loosely-worded statements can be forgiven in
hurried conversation, but not in writing, where the author has a
chance to revise and tighten. If you read carefully and retain
your essential honesty, you will probably do well in your
discussions of the writings of others.

As you work on literary papers, remember a couple of basic
requirements:

• Focus your paper on certain key questions or major points.
  Try to make clear early in your paper what you have to offer.
  Then, in the rest of your paper, concentrate on making that
  offer good to the reader.

• Keep the reader in close contact with the actual work. When
  you make general points, support them by referring directly to
  the work in front of you. Quote some actual words used by a

poet. Point to specific events in a story. Refer in detail to the actions and words of a character in a play.

Developing the Writing

A. Using a selection of literature studied this year, respond to three of the following topics. Write a paragraph for each of your three topics.
1. What is the author's opinion of modern society?
2. What does the author seem to say about human destiny?
3. What is the author's concept of a hero?
4. What is the significance of the title?
5. What is the relation of human beings to nature in this piece of writing?
6. How does the author sustain the reader's interest?
7. Write a detailed description of one major character, showing how the details of his or her appearance and actions reveal his or her significance in the piece of writing.
8. What types of conflict appear in this piece of writing? Illustrate each.

B. Choose a piece of writing (book, magazine article, story, editorial, play, poem, etc.) that moved you so much that you might naturally talk to a friend or classmate about it. Maybe you love it; maybe you hate it; maybe you have mixed feelings. But it hit you hard. Write several paragraphs telling why and how it affected you. Let the reader see what excited you about the writing.

This is not a book report. Don't try to summarize what you read. Don't try to cover everything in it.

C. Most narrative literary genres include the following elements: plot, characters, setting, and theme. A good way to evaluate the impact a literary work has had on you is to consider a series of questions about these elements. Consider the following questions with respect to the story *Appointment with Love*. Briefly jot down some answers.

1. **Plot**
   a. Is the plot believable?
   b. Do the events of the plot logically follow one another?
   c. Do I find the plot interesting and exciting?

2. **Character**
   a. How are the people characterized?
      • Physical appearance?
      • The opinions of other characters towards the individual?
      • What the character says and does?
      • What the character thinks and feels?
   b. Do I think the main characters are realistic?
   c. Do I sympathize with the main characters?

3. **Setting**
   a. What effects does the setting have on story events?
   b. Do I find that the setting is portrayed vividly enough?

4. **Theme**
   a. Do I feel that the theme offers a meaningful message about life?
   b. Do I agree with the theme?

D. Now incorporate comments about the above four elements into a short essay about the story *Appointment with Love.* Here is a simple outline you can follow:
• Introductory paragraph — Lead into a thesis statement saying that a plot summary and a discussion of characterization, setting, and theme will follow.
• First developmental paragraph — present a brief plot summary.
• Second developmental paragraph — discuss characterization.
• Third developmental paragraph — discuss setting.
• Fourth developmental paragraph — discuss the theme.
• Concluding paragraph — state what you particularly liked or disliked about the selection, and make some brief summarizing remarks.

Revising and Editing

Choose one piece of writing done in this chapter, and submit it to your teacher for evaluation.

Before doing so, evaluate it yourself, using the following questions.
• Did you avoid simply retelling the story? Instead, did you develop your topic or topics?
• Did you avoid straying off the point?

- Did you avoid too-long quotations in an attempt to fill up space? (Quotations should be supplements to your own thinking and writing, not substitutes.)

Make any improvements that seem necessary.

Growing from Writing

A major theme in many short stories and novels is the search by a character for "home," a place where he or she can find refuge and will feel secure and happy. Often the search involves a journey, sometimes brief, but at other times long and marked by many stages.

Discuss the search for "home" with reference to the main character in a story or novel you've read. How close does the character come to achieving his or her goal?

As you write, keep in mind and try to avoid the following two common mistakes that students often make when writing about literature.

- *The "I like it" mistake.* When you are asked to comment on a literary work, the assignment is intended to measure more than emotional intensity. It is usually aimed at finding out how well you understand the work and how logically you think.
- *The "it can mean anything" mistake.* It is true that a work of literature may validly mean one thing to one reader and something different to another. There is not one "right" meaning to any literary work. But just because there is not simply one meaning, all interpretations of a piece of literature are not valid. To interpret responsibly, you must be able to:
  - Specify the point of view you used in interpreting the literarary work.
  - Cite evidence from the text to support your interpretation of it.
  - Show the logical lines leading from the evidence in the text to your interpretation.

Classified Ads

I Found It in the Want Ads

Classified advertisements include information that readers need in order to purchase goods or services. Because such ads have to be written in as few words as possible, they give you good practice in writing briefly. You must get all your facts in and try to persuade the reader to act — while at the same time paying as little as possible for the publication of your ad.

NEW IN TOWN? Call us about this beautiful home on large treed lot, 3 bedrooms, solid brick construction. Quiet street near schools, churches, public transportation, Bender Shopping Centre. Carolyn Franklin 861-8321.

PIZZA driver required. Must have own car. 469-1128.

NEEDED IMMEDIATELY teenage babysitter for 2 children, ages 7 and 9. Must be reliable, non-smoker. Redwing School Area. After 5 — 434-8553.

I LOST WEIGHT. So can you. Join the Lose Phat Phast Club. Call Phil or Phyllis — 434-5849.

GROUP GUITAR LESSONS. Reasonable rates, evenings, Kiwanis building. Call B. Tremblay 422-2244.

BUILDING A WRITING CONTEXT

1. **Which ads have the most impact?**
2. **Which ads have a personal touch?**
3. **Is there an ad you would respond to? Why?**
4. **What makes some ads stand out from others?**

THE WRITING WORKSHOP

Preparing to Write

Examine several examples of classified ads in newspapers and magazines. Notice how they make their point quickly and succinctly. Because the writer must pay by the number of words used, classified ads are usually as brief as possible.

When you read the classified section of a newspaper or magazine, you often see ads under headings such as *Homes for Sale, Jobs Wanted, Lost and Found, Automobiles, Educational Courses, Services, Pets, Lonely Hearts*. What similar headings have you seen?

Developing the Writing

1. Work in a small group. As a group, decide upon a magazine that would accept classified ads. Perhaps it could be a sports magazine, a teen magazine, a pet magazine, a motor magazine, a home and garden magazine, or a fashion magazine. As a group, you are responsible for writing the classified ads pages that might appear in the magazine.
2. In preparing your ads page, you will have to decide:
   • What kinds of classified ads would appear in your magazine?
   • Would you have different headings for different types of ads?
   • What captions could you use to capture the readers' attention for the various advertisements?
   • What essential information needs to appear in each ad?
   • Given extra cost, what information could you afford to add?
   • How do you want readers to respond to each ad? For example, should they write, phone, or appear in person?
3. Work together as a group to create a page of classified ads for your magazine. Questions that an interested reader might have should be answered in each ad. However, since every word costs money, you will have to choose your words carefully.

4. Consider:
- Which words should be in large or bold print?
- Which pieces of information should appear first in the ad?
- What information can be eliminated from the ad but could be given later by phone or letter?
- Is a phone number or address going to be published?

Revising and Editing

Exchange ad pages with another group. Each group member chooses two ads from among those written by the other group. He or she then writes comments on how the ads could be improved.

Now exchange ad pages again. Taking the comments into consideration, the group who wrote the ads improves them in any ways that seem suitable.

Sharing and Publishing

Post all the ad pages on a wall or bulletin board. Each member of the class then chooses one ad and responds to it. Depending on what the ad says, the response may take the form of:
- A letter.
- A telephone call. (Role-play it for the class and/or write out the dialogue.)
- A meeting between the interested person and the person who placed the ad. (Role-play it for the class and/or write out the dialogue.)

Growing from Writing

A. Think of four items in your house. Prepare four classified ads that might appear in the newspaper in order to sell these items. Make the items sound appealing without writing too much, since you will want to keep your cost down.

B. Create a Classified Ads section for a newspaper of the future. What kinds of items will be sold 200 years from now? What kinds of jobs will be advertised 200 years from now? What kinds of homes will be for sale?

C. Create a classified ad for "the perfect friend." For this ad, cost is no problem, so you can list all the qualities you wish.

Instead of writing an ad for the perfect friend, you might wish to write it for one of the following: the perfect brother, the perfect sister, the perfect boss, the perfect babysitter.

Technical Writing

How Does Your Garden Grow?

"A thing of beauty is a joy forever."

John Keats

Little touches of beauty in our homes often mean more than we realize. You can help beautify your home; for example, with a windowsill garden of house plants. But don't try to do too much at once — start on a modest level. Read the following article, for example, and learn one way to have fragrant spring bulbs blooming as early as February.

Growing Bulbs EILEEN TOTTEN

What you need

A bulb	Bulb fibre or peat
A plant pot	Water
A pebble	A large bowl

Start at first with one bulb in a simple pot. Choose your bulb in September and plant it right away if you want results around February. You can choose hyacinth, crocus, or snowdrop bulbs. All of these will grow well in a pot or bowl. A daffodil bulb on its own will not make a very good show.

You need the large bowl I have mentioned for mixing the fibre or sedge peat in water. It might be a good idea to spread newspaper on the table or floor before you do this. Pour the water, little by little, on to the fibre or peat and mix it together with your hands. It will be ready when you can squeeze a few drops of water out of it.

If you use a clay pot for your bulb you will need to put a pebble or small piece of broken pot over the drainage hole. You can put a few dry leaves on top of this, and then pack in fibre halfway up the pot.

Now it is time to plant the bulb. Put it on the fibre, so its top, the pointed end, just sticks up level with the rim of the pot. Then pack more fibre tightly round the bulb till the pot is almost full. The peat or fibre should reach to about 1.3 cm from the rim of the pot. Water the bulb well.

Now is the time when the bulb must go away in the dark for eight or ten weeks. It needs this time to grow strong roots before it starts flowering. A good place might be a cupboard which is not used too often, or an attic where you can put a box over the pot to keep the light out. Make sure it is a cool place that you choose, too. Don't keep looking at the bulb, or you will let the light in. But do water it from time to time. Feel the fibre to see if it is too dry.

After ten weeks, your bulb should show a strong shoot just over 2.5 cm long. You can bring the pot into the daylight now and put it on a windowsill. Make sure the bulb gets plenty of light, but not too much heat. The bulb should grow slowly and not be forced. Never put it beside a fire, for instance.

Water the bulbs so that the fibre or peat is always moist. And turn the plant round once a week so it won't lean over one way to get to the sunlight. When it starts to flower, you can push a little stick into the fibre. Then tie the flower stalk loosely to it, to support it.

BUILDING A WRITING CONTEXT

1. **Why was it a good idea for the author to begin by listing the things needed? In what other pieces of writing have you seen this done?**
2. **What words does the author use to help readers follow the time sequence of the process she is describing.**

THE WRITING WORKSHOP

Preparing to Write

Today we seem to be reading an increasing amount of technical writing. If we buy a computer or microwave oven, we read books and manuals on its use and maintenance. If someone makes a great medical discovery, we often read the technical details in the newspaper. In our rapidly changing world, you may find yourself not only doing a lot of technical *reading* but also *writing*. Here are a few guidelines for this kind of writing.

1. Avoid jargon whenever possible. For example, don't use the word *dichotomy* when the word *split* would do.
2. Avoid abstract nouns when you can. For example, instead of writing: *Solution took place,* say more simply: *The crystals dissolved.*
3. Avoid long words that are pompous or vague. For example, do not say *entertainment value* when you mean simply *fun.*
4. Do not pack too many ideas into one sentence.
5. Do not move on to a new topic or fact until you have given your reader enough information to help him or her absorb the first topic or fact.
6. Include diagrams, tables, graphs, and charts when appropriate. They can often help you clarify ideas and information for the reader.

Developing the Writing

A. Write a short article explaining one of the following processes. Include all the necessary steps (in a numbered list if you wish). Present the steps in order, and develop each with sufficient details.

1. Using a cash register.
2. Growing a specific type of flower, fruit, or vegetable in a home garden.
3. Using a pocket calculator.
4. Treating a bite from a poisonous snake.
5. Gripping a golf club.
6. Training a dog (or some other pet).
7. Potting an indoor plant.
8. Changing the oil in an automobile.

142

9. Serving a tennis ball.
10. Baking muffins.
11. Carrying out some other process with which you're familiar.

B. Computer programs are sometimes based on flowcharts. A flowchart is a diagram showing steps to be taken in carrying out some process or solving some problem. Example:

How to Put on a Sock

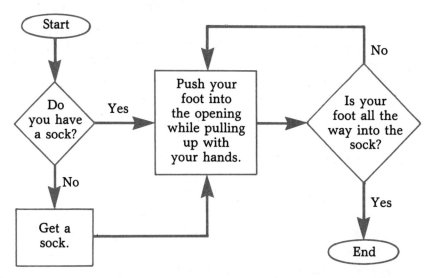

Since a computer knows nothing at all without being told, instructions must be broken down into simple steps. When programming a computer, you can't take common sense for granted, as you can when giving directions to human beings.

Make a flowchart explaining one of the following processes. Use symbols as in the flowchart above; for example, rectangle for instruction, diamond for question.
• How to drink a glass of water.
• How to feed a dog (or cat).
• How to put on a hat.
• How to turn on a lamp.
• How to plant a radish seed.
• How to pull a weed.

C. Write a short article to include in a newspaper or popular scientific magazine in the year 2000. What new invention or scientific discovery might be making news by the year 2000? Write about it.

Revising and Editing

Reread one or more pieces of writing you did in this chapter, making improvements based on the following questions.
1. Are my sentences written in clear, simple language?
2. Am I sure of the meanings of the words I used?
3. Have I carelessly left out any words?
4. Have I become "windy," cluttering my writing with excess words?
5. Have I used punctuation properly to prevent confusion or misreading?
6. Have I explained the meanings of terms that my reader might not understand?

Sharing and Publishing

Give one piece of writing done in this chapter to a younger student to read. Can he or she easily follow your ideas? Talk about your writing with the younger student. Can you make further improvements based on this discussion?

Growing from Writing

Try the following "Robot Project."
1. Design a robot. Draw it and give it a name.
2. Jot down notes on the following:
   • What is it made of and how does it function?
   • What can it do? What limitations does it have?
   • What innovations have you included? What is unique about your robot?
3. Use your notes to write a brochure introducing your robot to a potential buyer. Include illustrations.

REVISION CHECKLISTS

Content Checklist

1. Will my writing interest my readers?
2. Did I say everything I wanted to say?
3. Did I say it the way I wanted to say it?
4. Did I say it clearly so that others will understand what I wrote?
5. Did I stay on topic throughout my piece of writing?
6. Did I include all the necessary information?
7. Should I leave some ideas out?
8. Should I change some of my ideas?
9. Did I write the events, ideas, and/or steps in a logical order?
10. If I was asked to follow a pattern, did I do it well?
11. Did I use comparisons when appropriate to make my work more interesting and more accurate?
12. Did I write a good beginning, middle, and end?
13. If writing a paragraph, did I write a strong topic sentence? Do all the sentences in the paragraph belong with the topic sentence? Did I write an effective closing sentence? Did I organize the sentences in the best order?
14. Did I vary my sentence types and constructions?
15. Did I use the most accurate and interesting words that I could think of?

Proofreading Checklist

1. Does each sentence make sense?
2. Does the order of words in each sentence make sense?
3. If a sentence is too long, how can I change it to make two or more shorter sentences? If some sentences are too short, how can I combine them?
4. Is my grammar correct?
5. Have I punctuated each sentence correctly?
6. Have I used capital letters correctly?
7. Where I have used direct speech, have I punctuated it correctly?
8. Did I spell words correctly, checking those about which I was unsure?
9. Did I use proper form with regard to indenting, titles, and margins?
10. Is my writing clear and easy to read?

Author/Title Index

Subject Index

148

Acknowledgments

Every effort has been made to acknowledge all sources of material used in this book. The publishers would be grateful if any errors or omissions were pointed out, so that they may be corrected.

Acknowledgment is gratefully made for the use of the following copyright material: "Not Next Door to Me, He Isn't" from *Language and Learning* by James Britton (Allen Lane, The Penguin Press, 1970), pp. 147-149, copyright © James Britton, 1970. Reprinted by permission of Penguin Books Ltd., London. "A Strange Visitor" by Robert Zend © 1985 by Janine Zend. "The Dinner Party" by Mona Gardner. © 1942 Saturday Review magazine. Reprinted by permission. Excerpt from "Wormlore" by Betty Roots from *Zap Underground*. Reprinted by permission of Fitzhenry & Whiteside Ltd. "Dream comes true for Brian — Canadiens' unlikely hero sets a record in overtime" by Tony Fitz-Gerald reprinted by permission of The Hamilton Spectator. "Jays find the Key to winning ways" by Jeff Dickens reprinted by permission of The Hamilton Spectator. "Dan George, A Noble Man" from *Canadians All 1: Portraits of Our People*, Terry Angus & Shirley White editors, © 1976 Methuen Publications (A Division of the Carswell Company Ltd.). "Fog" from *Chicago Poems* by Carl Sandburg, copyright 1916 by Holt, Rinehart and Winston, Inc.; renewed 1944 by Carl Sandburg. Reprinted by permission of Harcourt Brace Jovanovich, Inc. "How to Eat a Poem" from *It Doesn't Always Have to Rhyme* by Eve Merriam. Copyright © 1964 by Eve Merriam. All rights reserved. Reprinted by permission of Marian Reiner for the author. "Kittens" by Katherine Anastasio. Reprinted by permission of the author. "The Shark" by E.J. Pratt. Reprinted by permission of University of Toronto Press. "Rubik's Cube" by Paul Salvo. Reprinted by permission of the author. Limerick by Christopher Tihor. Reprinted by permission of the author. "Dreams" from *The Dream Keeper and Other Poems*, by Langston Hughes. Copyright 1932 by Alfred A. Knopf, Inc. and renewed 1960 by Langston Hughes. Reprinted by permission of the publisher. "Steam Shovel" from *Upper Pastures* by Charles Malam. Reprinted by permission of Henry Holt and Company. Advertising for Lennox Collections, leading direct response marketer of porcelain and crystal collectibles. The Manhattan Ocean Club advertisement. Agency: Angotti, Thomas, Hedge, Inc. Client: New York Restaurant Group, Inc. Writer: Tom Thomas. Art Director: Anthony Angotti. "'Fuzzy' Math Is More Human" reprinted by permission of The Green & White, University of Saskatchewan. "The Effort to Save Animals" reprinted from *The How and Why Wonder Book of Extinct Animals*, Price/Stern/Sloan Publishers Inc., Los Angeles. Copyright by John Burton. All rights reserved. "Growing Bulbs" from *Sow and Grow* by Eileen Totten. Reprinted by permission of Bell & Hyman Publishers, London.